Sock Monkey

SOCK MONKEY

THE "INCHES" INCIDENT

WRITTEN AND DRAWN BY

TONY MILLIONAIRE

Dark Horse Books®

EDITOR
Dave Land

ASSISTANT EDITOR
Katie Moody

DESIGNER
Tony Ong

ART DIRECTOR
Lia Ribacchi

PUBLISHER
Mike Richardson

SOCK MONKEY: THE "INCHES" INCIDENT

This book collects issues one through four of the Dark Horse comic-book series
Sock Monkey: The "Inches" Incident.

Published by
Dark Horse Books
A division of Dark Horse Comics, Inc.
10956 SE Main Street
Milwaukie, OR 97222

darkhorse.com

To find a comic shop in your area, call the Comic Shop Locator Service
toll-free at 1-888-266-4226.

First edition: September 2007
ISBN: 978-1-59307-842-3

1 3 5 7 9 10 8 6 4 2

PRINTED IN CANADA

For Alice

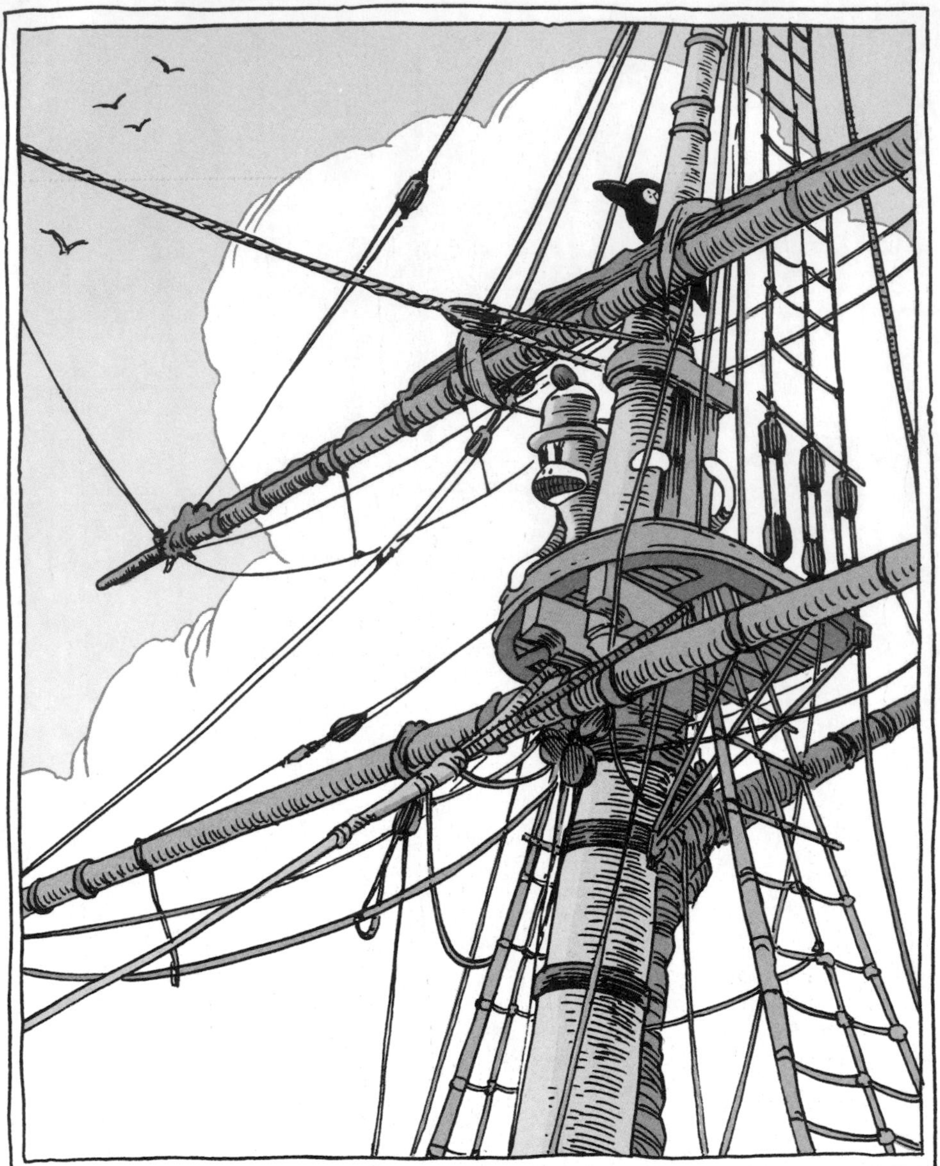

Chapter One

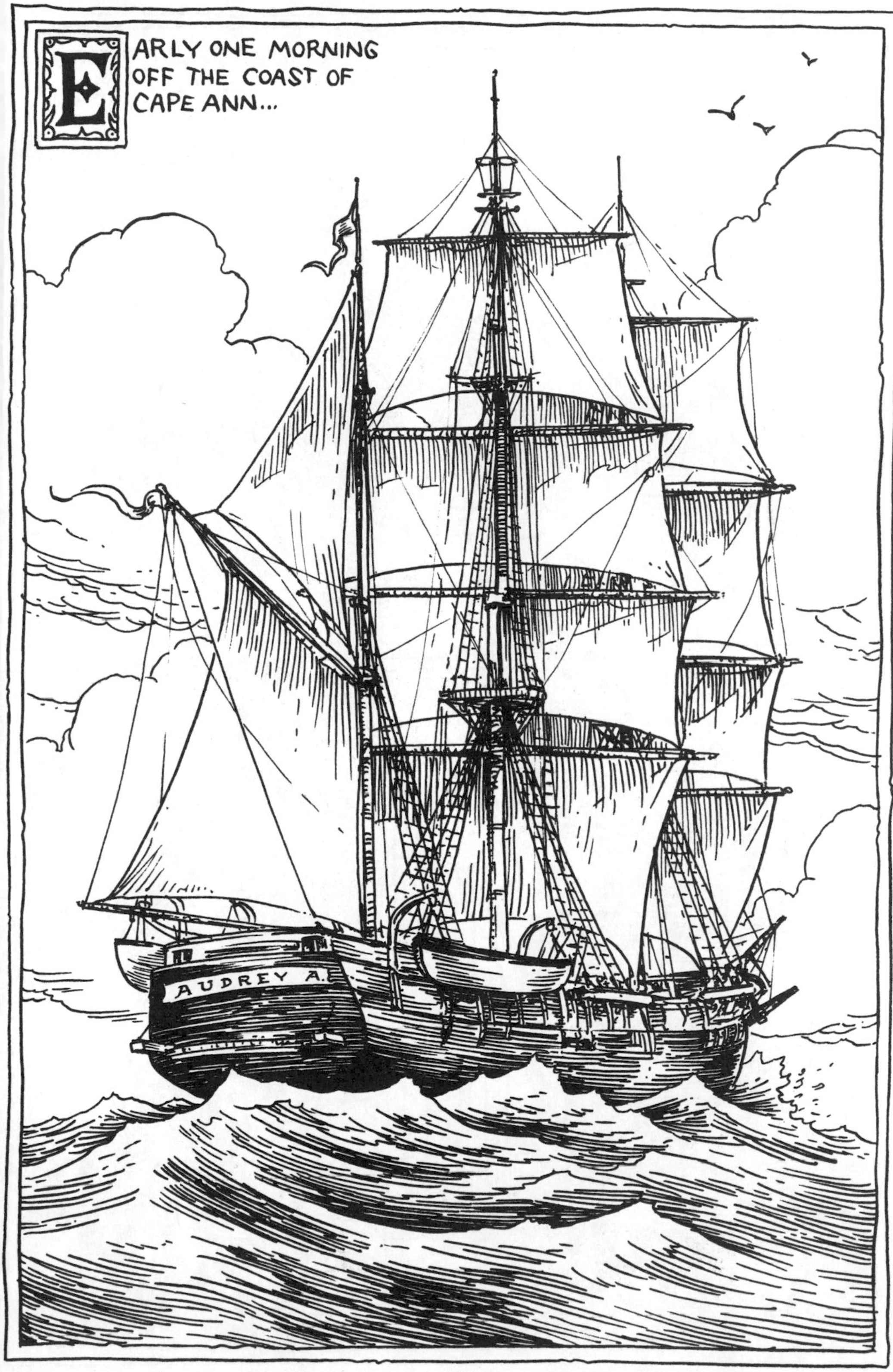
EARLY ONE MORNING OFF THE COAST OF CAPE ANN...
AUDREY A.

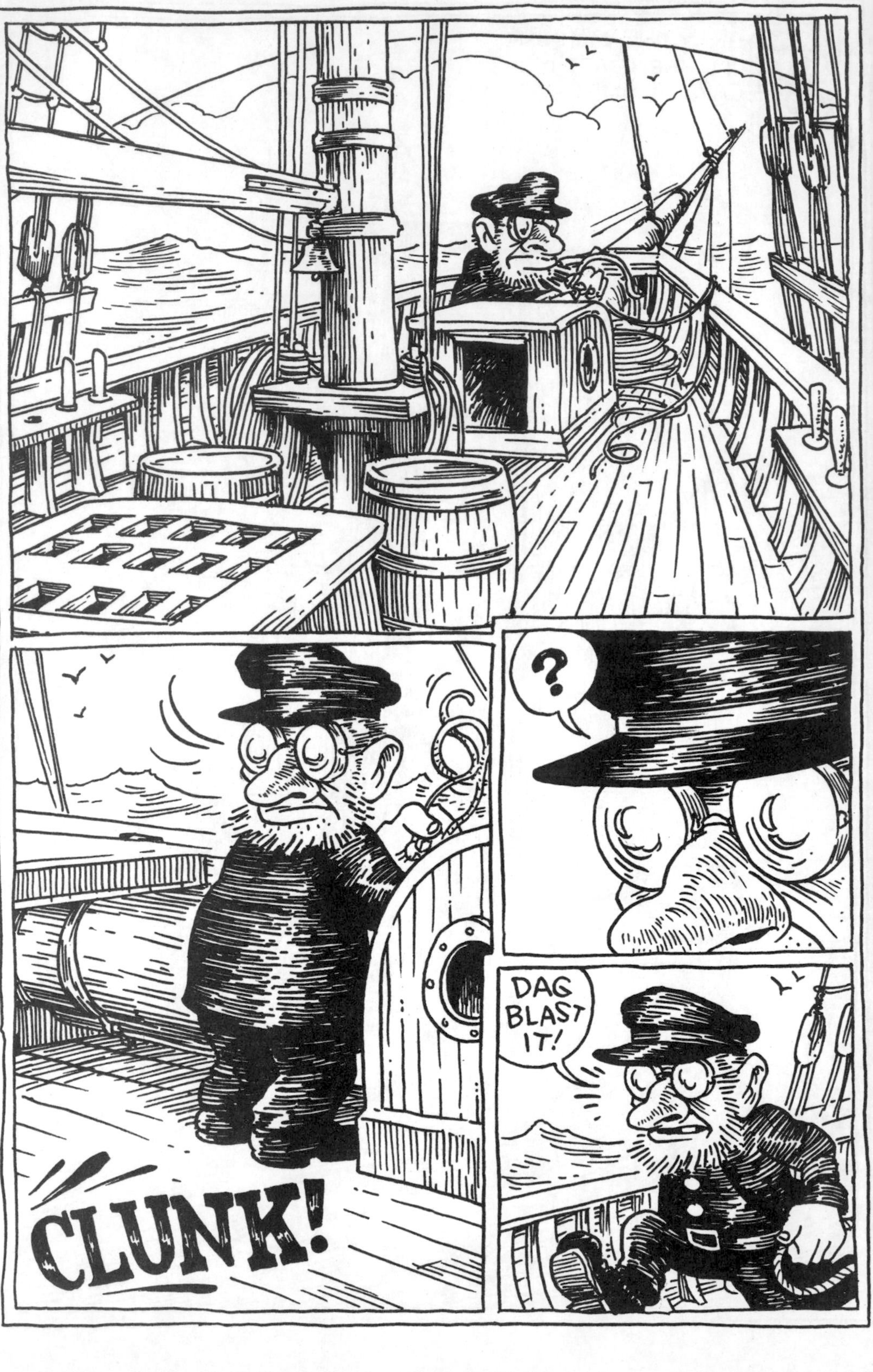
CLUNK!
?
DAG BLAST IT!

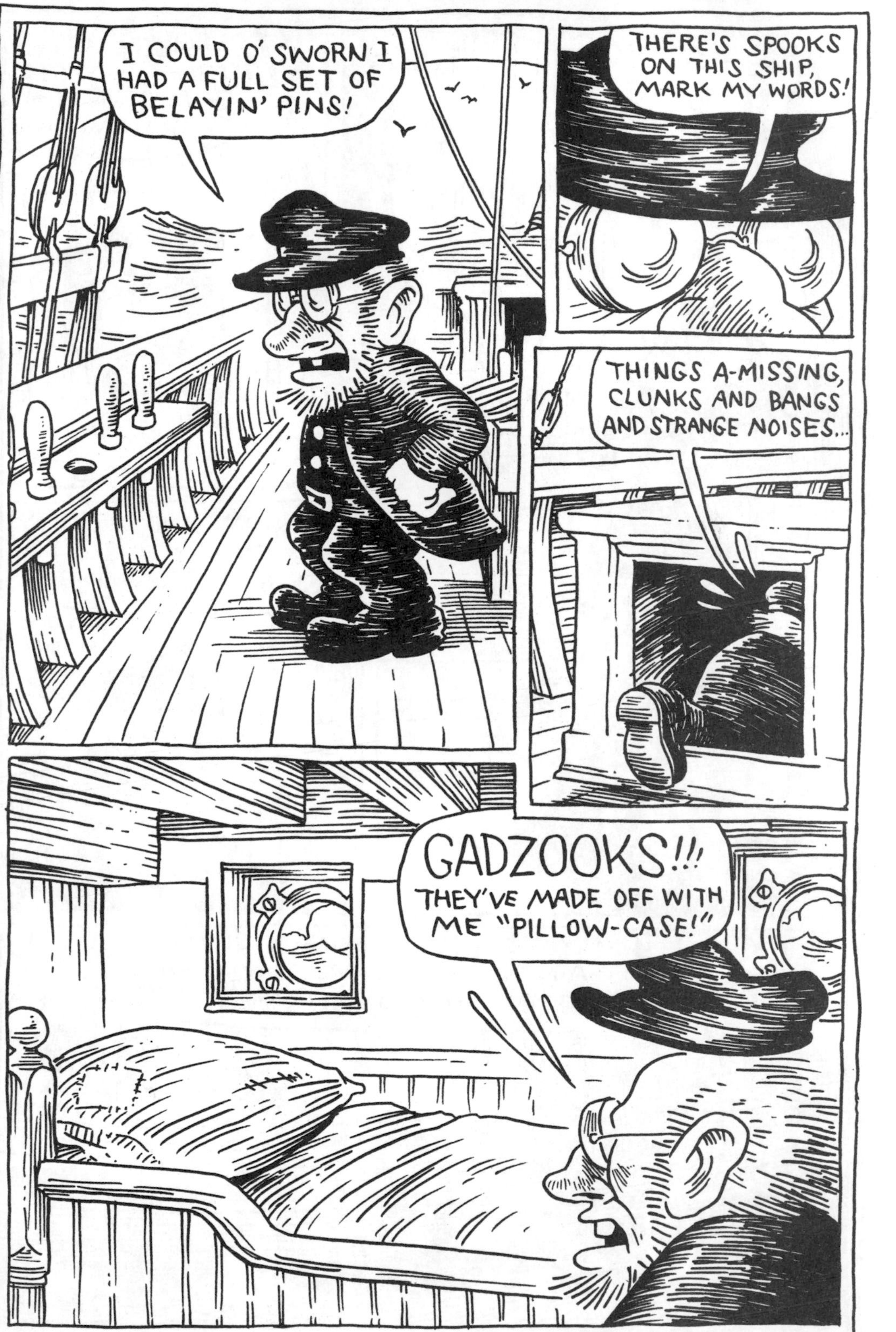
I COULD O' SWORN I HAD A FULL SET OF BELAYIN' PINS!
THERE'S SPOOKS ON THIS SHIP, MARK MY WORDS!
THINGS A-MISSING, CLUNKS AND BANGS AND STRANGE NOISES...
GADZOOKS!!! THEY'VE MADE OFF WITH ME "PILLOW-CASE!"

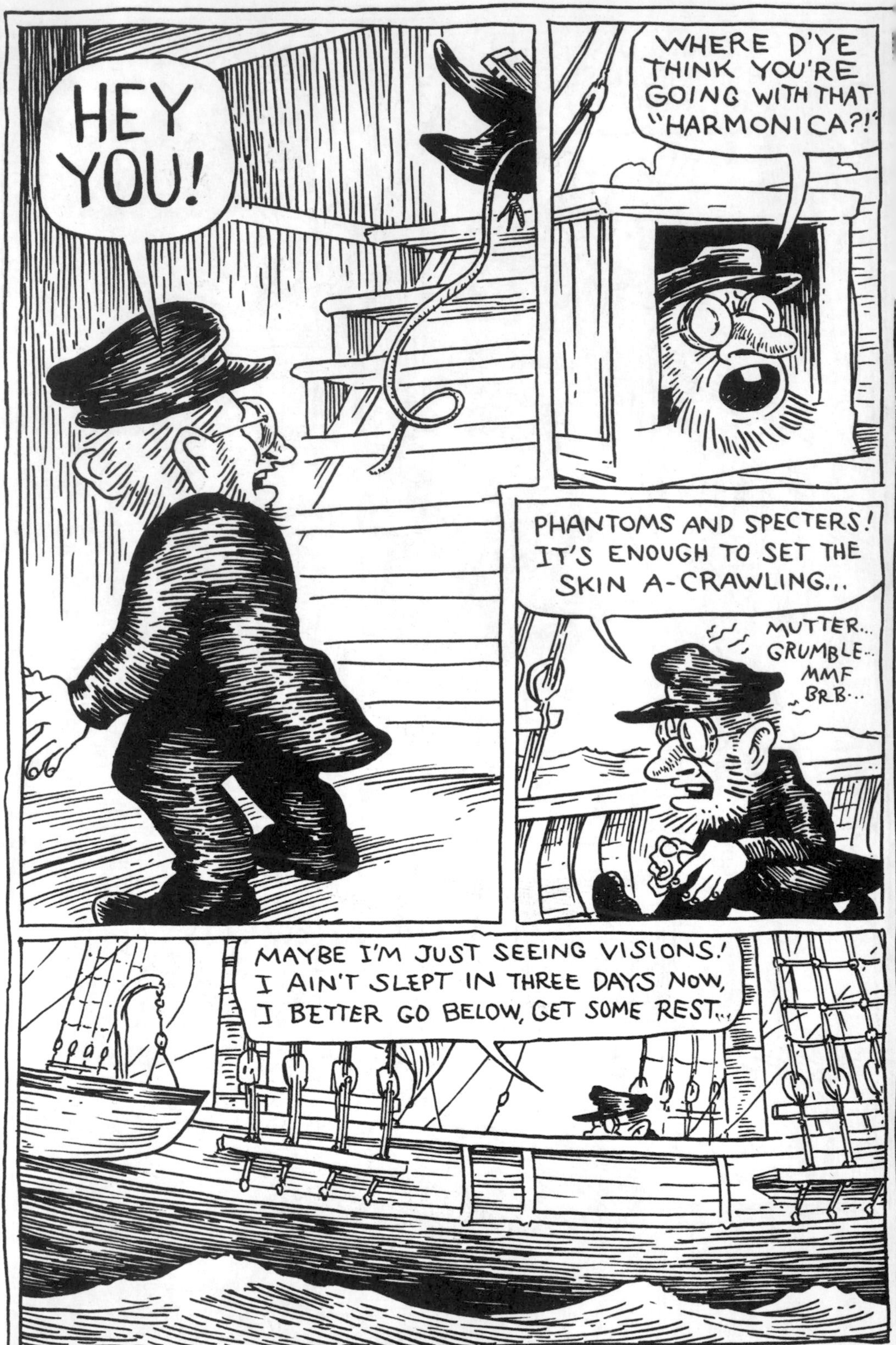
HEY YOU!
WHERE D'YE THINK YOU'RE GOING WITH THAT "HARMONICA?!"
PHANTOMS AND SPECTERS! IT'S ENOUGH TO SET THE SKIN A-CRAWLING...
MUTTER... GRUMBLE... MMF BRB...
MAYBE I'M JUST SEEING VISIONS! I AIN'T SLEPT IN THREE DAYS NOW, I BETTER GO BELOW, GET SOME REST...

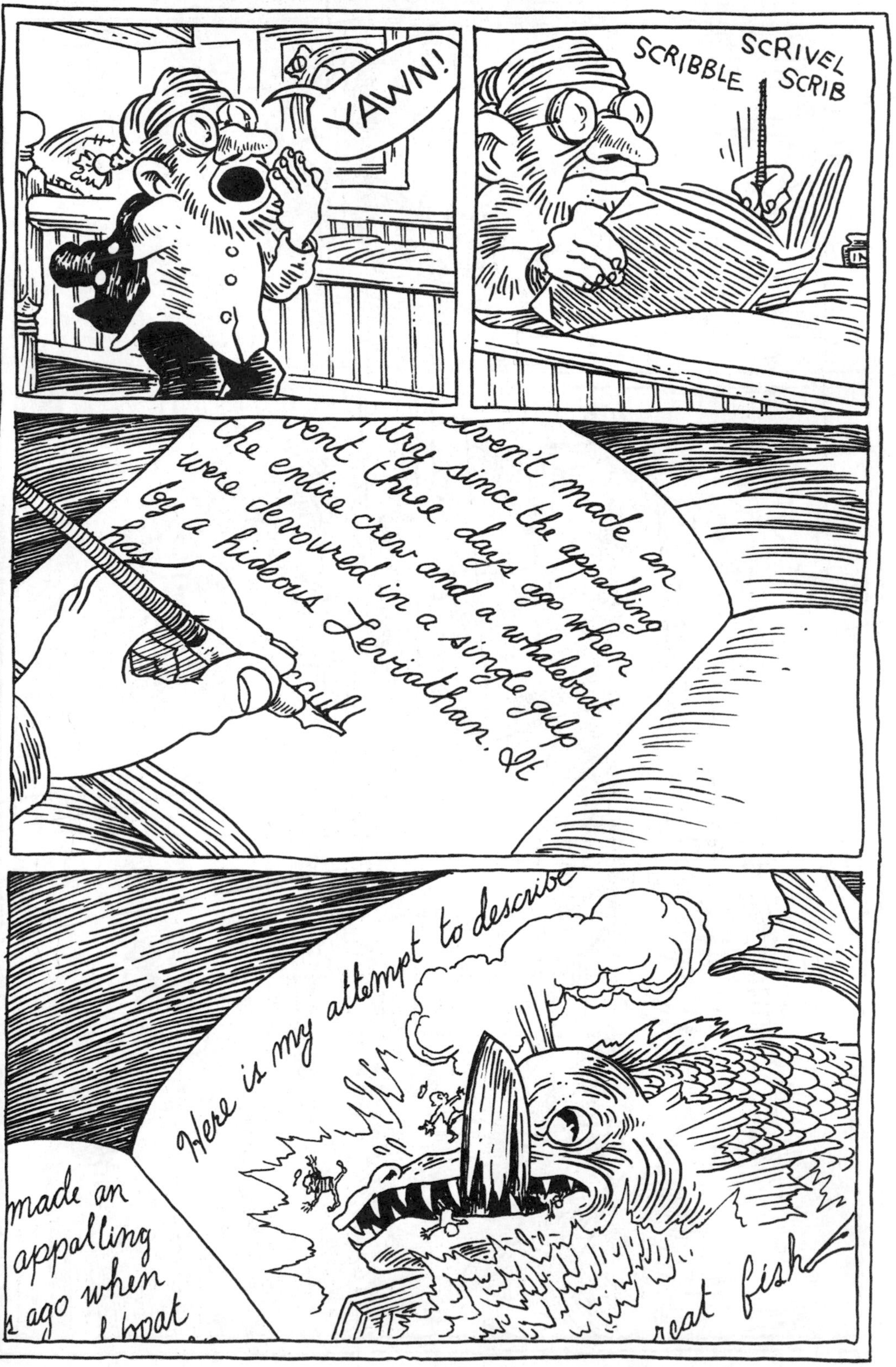
YAWN!
SCRIBBLE SCRIVEL SCRIB
...entry. I haven't made an ...vent since the appalling ...the entire crew and a whaleboat were devoured in a single gulp by a hideous Leviathan. It has
Here is my attempt to describe
made an appalling ...s ago when ...boat
...reat fish

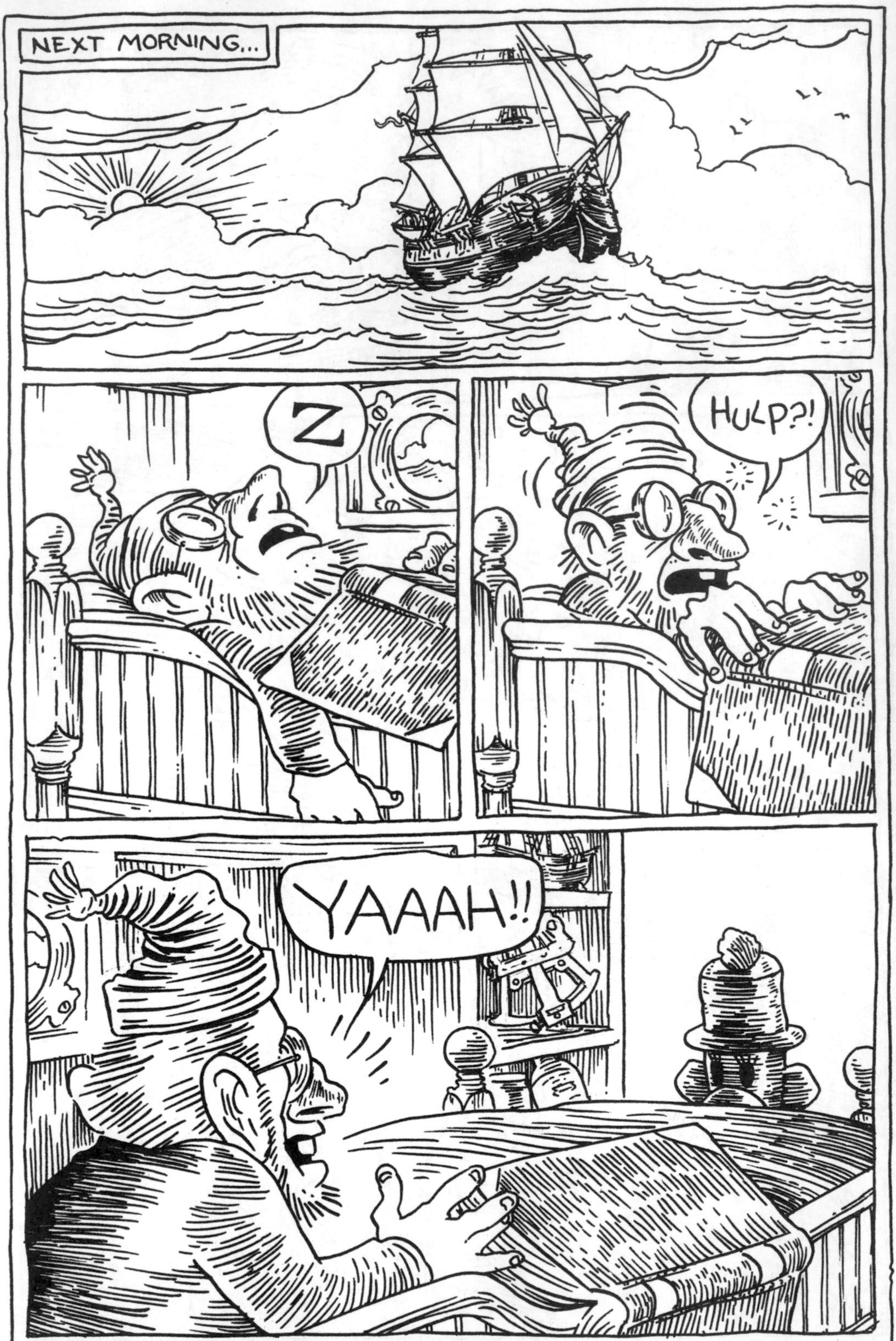
NEXT MORNING...
Z
HULP?!
YAAAH!!

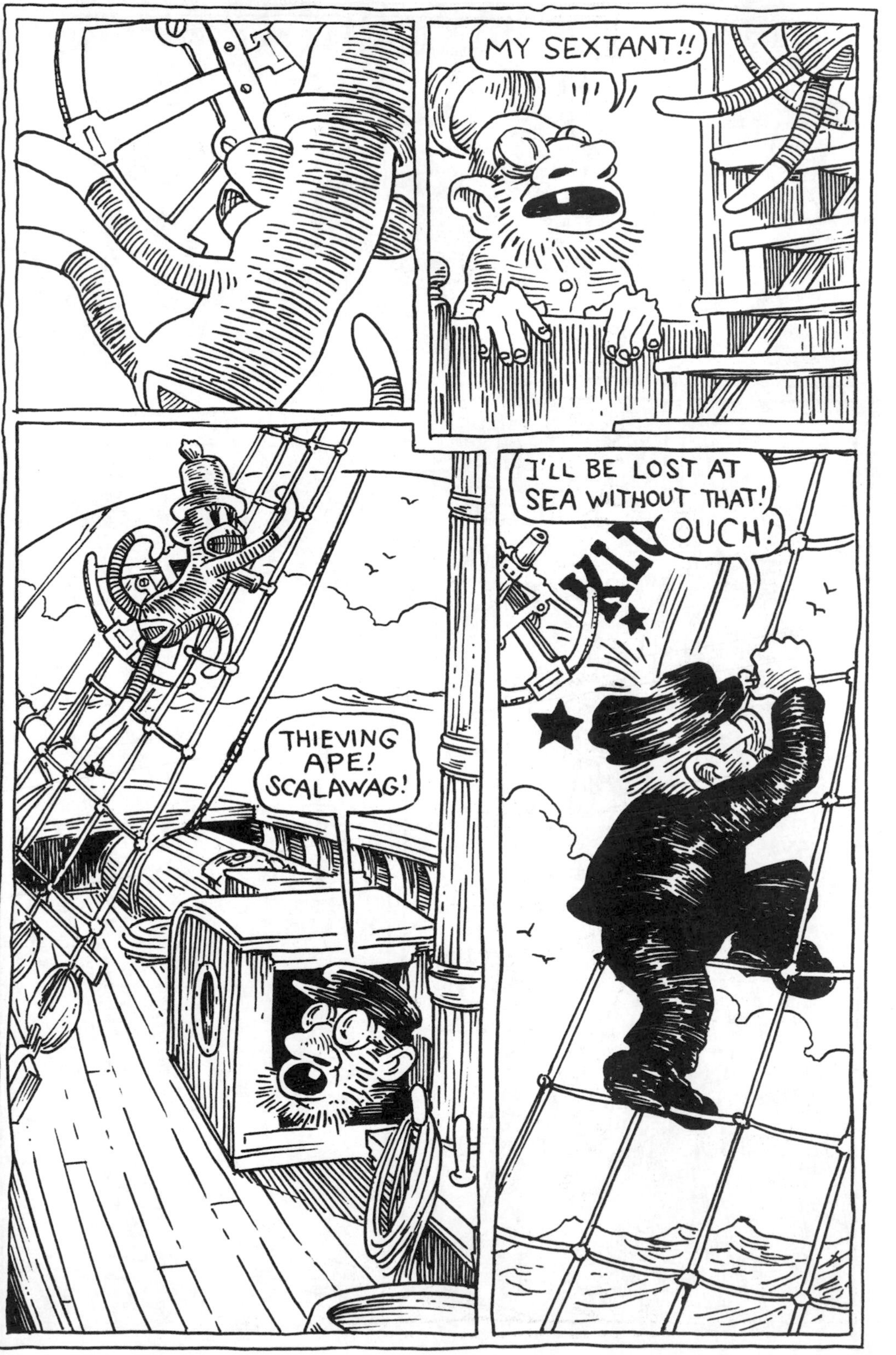
MY SEXTANT!!
THIEVING APE! SCALAWAG!
I'LL BE LOST AT SEA WITHOUT THAT!
KLU
OUCH!

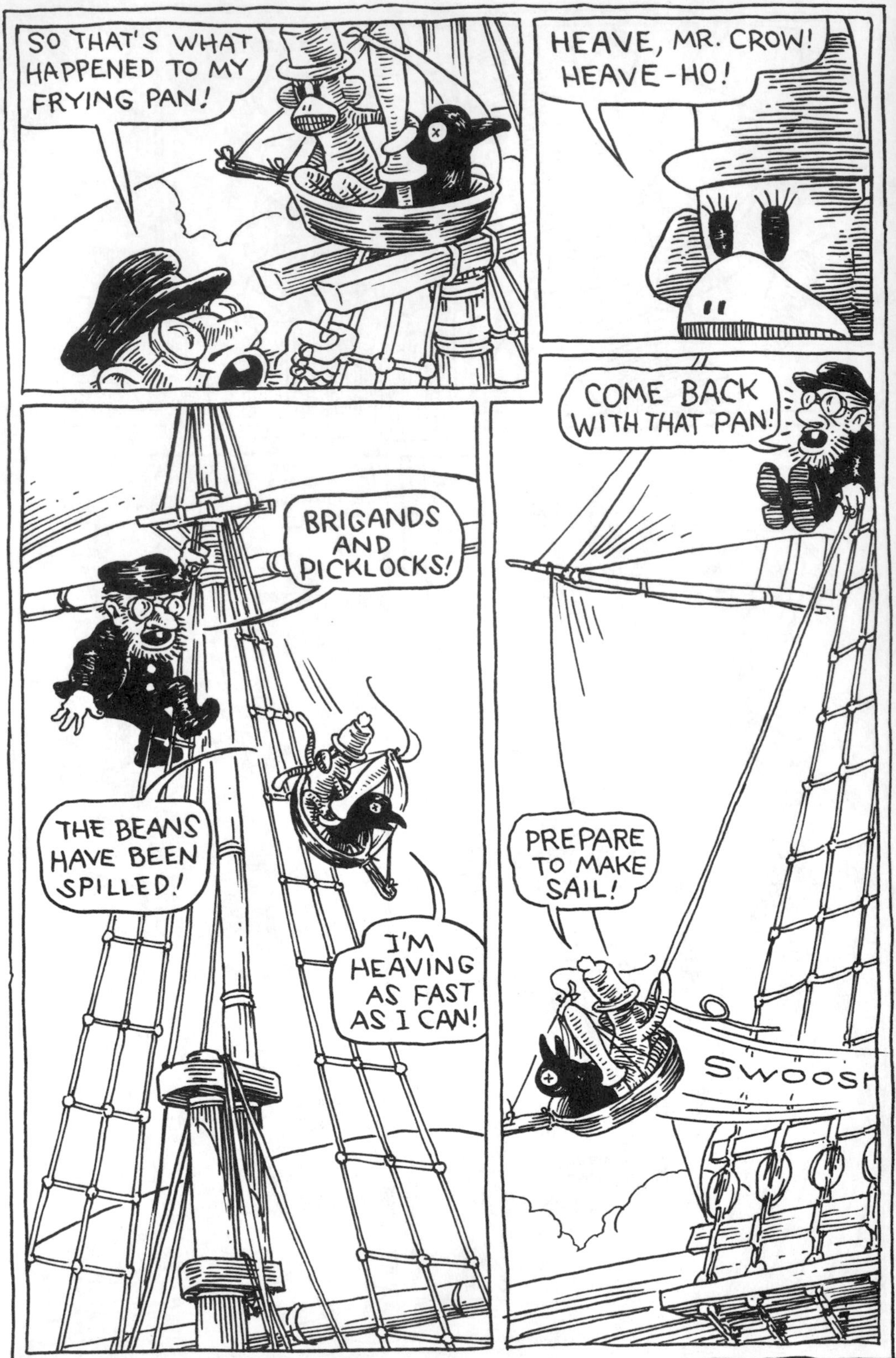
SO THAT'S WHAT HAPPENED TO MY FRYING PAN!
HEAVE, MR. CROW! HEAVE-HO!
BRIGANDS AND PICKLOCKS!
THE BEANS HAVE BEEN SPILLED!
I'M HEAVING AS FAST AS I CAN!
COME BACK WITH THAT PAN!
PREPARE TO MAKE SAIL!
SWOOSH

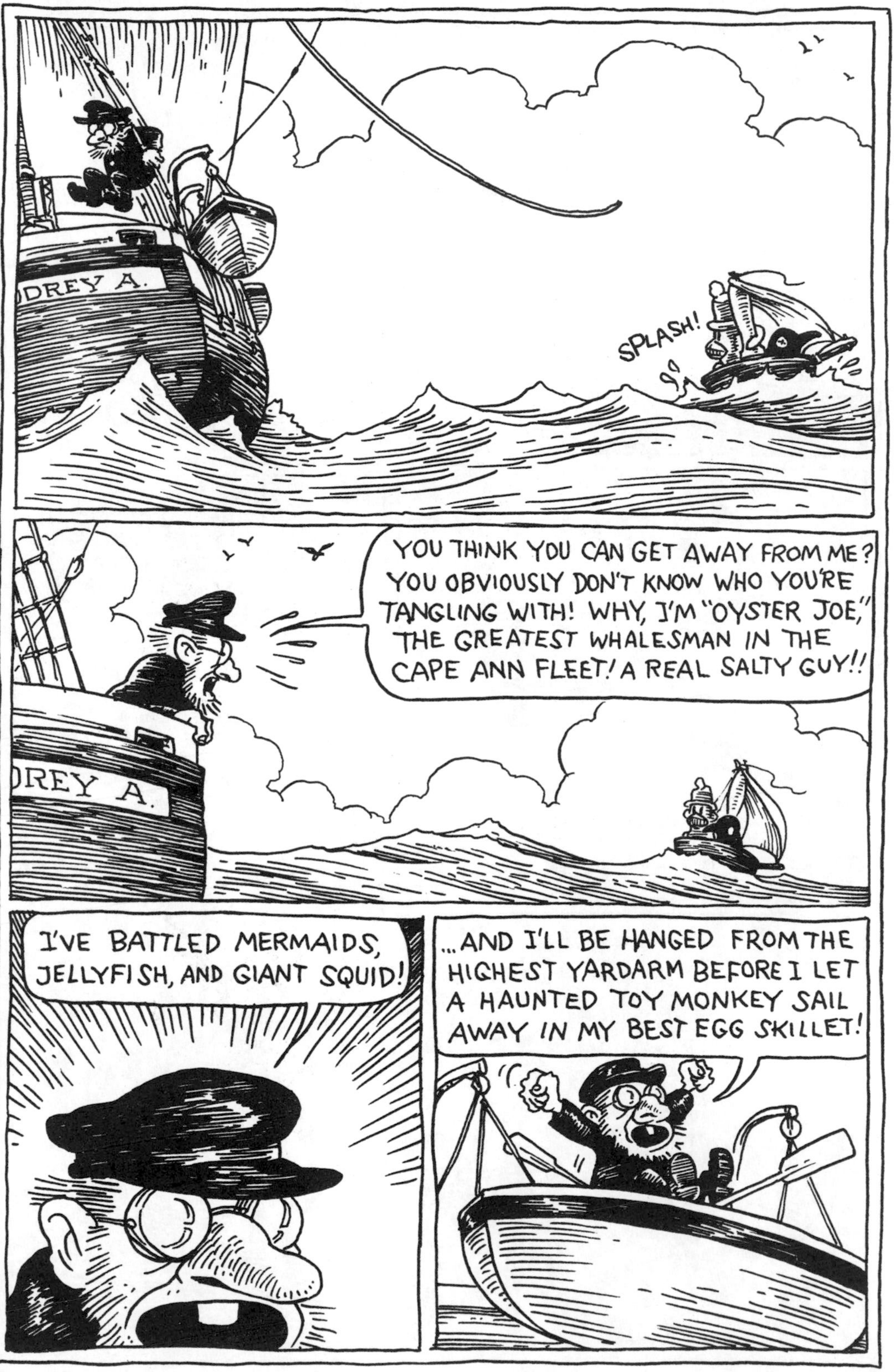

DREY A.
SPLASH!
YOU THINK YOU CAN GET AWAY FROM ME? YOU OBVIOUSLY DON'T KNOW WHO YOU'RE TANGLING WITH! WHY, I'M "OYSTER JOE," THE GREATEST WHALESMAN IN THE CAPE ANN FLEET! A REAL SALTY GUY!!
DREY A.
I'VE BATTLED MERMAIDS, JELLYFISH, AND GIANT SQUID!
...AND I'LL BE HANGED FROM THE HIGHEST YARDARM BEFORE I LET A HAUNTED TOY MONKEY SAIL AWAY IN MY BEST EGG SKILLET!

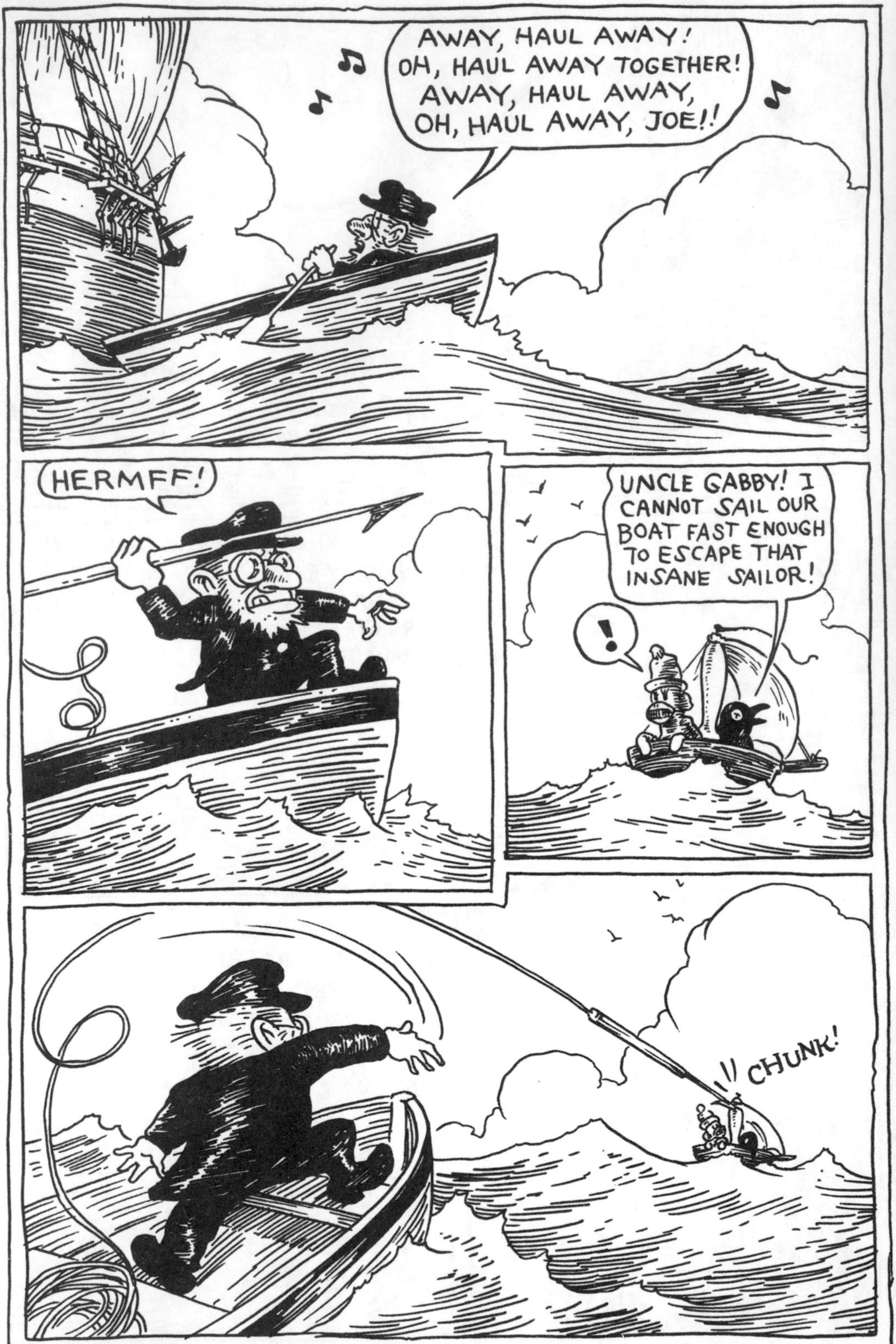
AWAY, HAUL AWAY! OH, HAUL AWAY TOGETHER! AWAY, HAUL AWAY, OH, HAUL AWAY, JOE!!
HERMFF!
!
UNCLE GABBY! I CANNOT SAIL OUR BOAT FAST ENOUGH TO ESCAPE THAT INSANE SAILOR!
CHUNK!

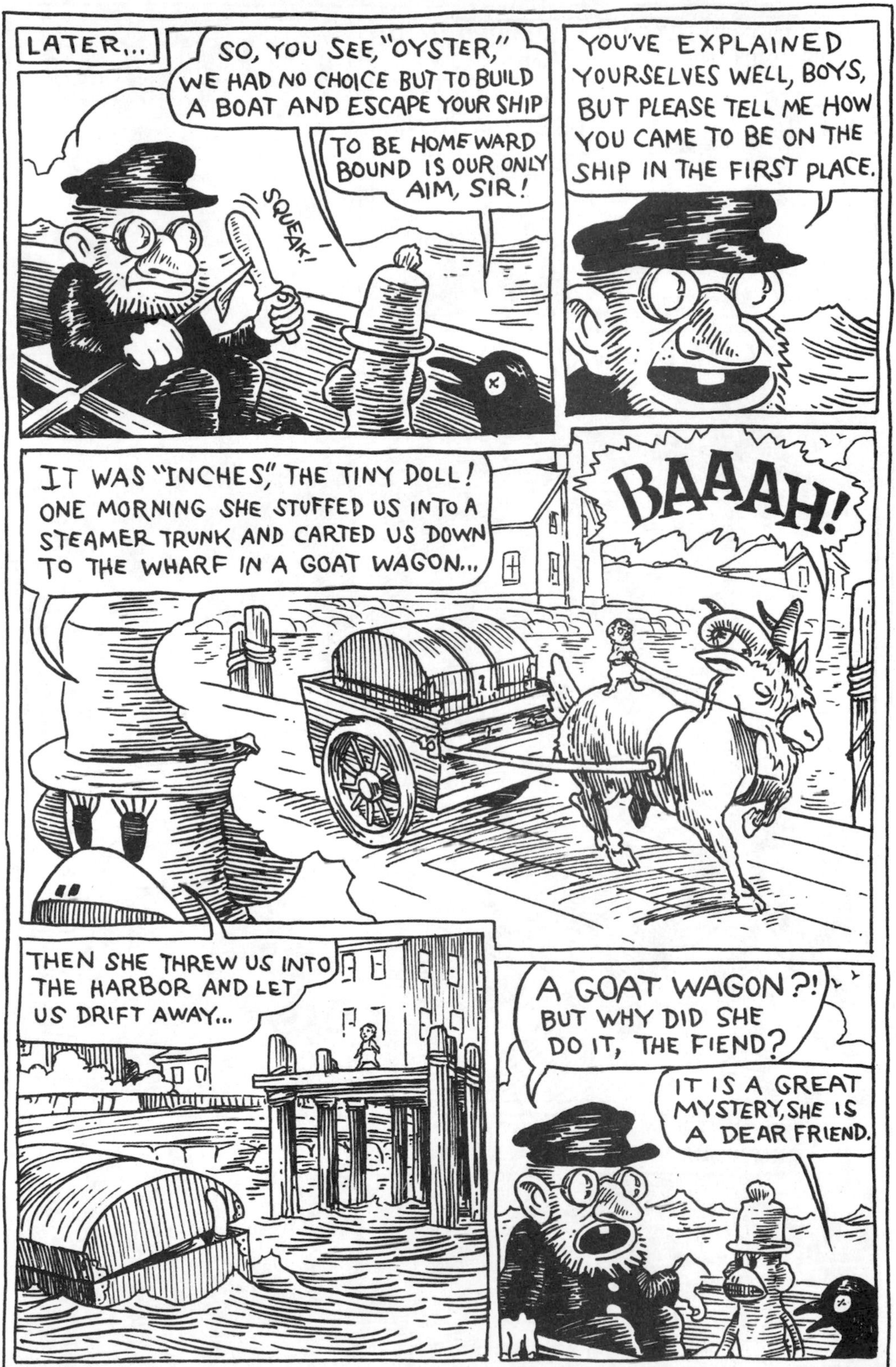
LATER...
SO, YOU SEE, "OYSTER," WE HAD NO CHOICE BUT TO BUILD A BOAT AND ESCAPE YOUR SHIP
TO BE HOMEWARD BOUND IS OUR ONLY AIM, SIR!
SQUEAK!
YOU'VE EXPLAINED YOURSELVES WELL, BOYS, BUT PLEASE TELL ME HOW YOU CAME TO BE ON THE SHIP IN THE FIRST PLACE.
IT WAS "INCHES," THE TINY DOLL! ONE MORNING SHE STUFFED US INTO A STEAMER TRUNK AND CARTED US DOWN TO THE WHARF IN A GOAT WAGON...
BAAAH!
THEN SHE THREW US INTO THE HARBOR AND LET US DRIFT AWAY...
A GOAT WAGON?! BUT WHY DID SHE DO IT, THE FIEND?
IT IS A GREAT MYSTERY, SHE IS A DEAR FRIEND.

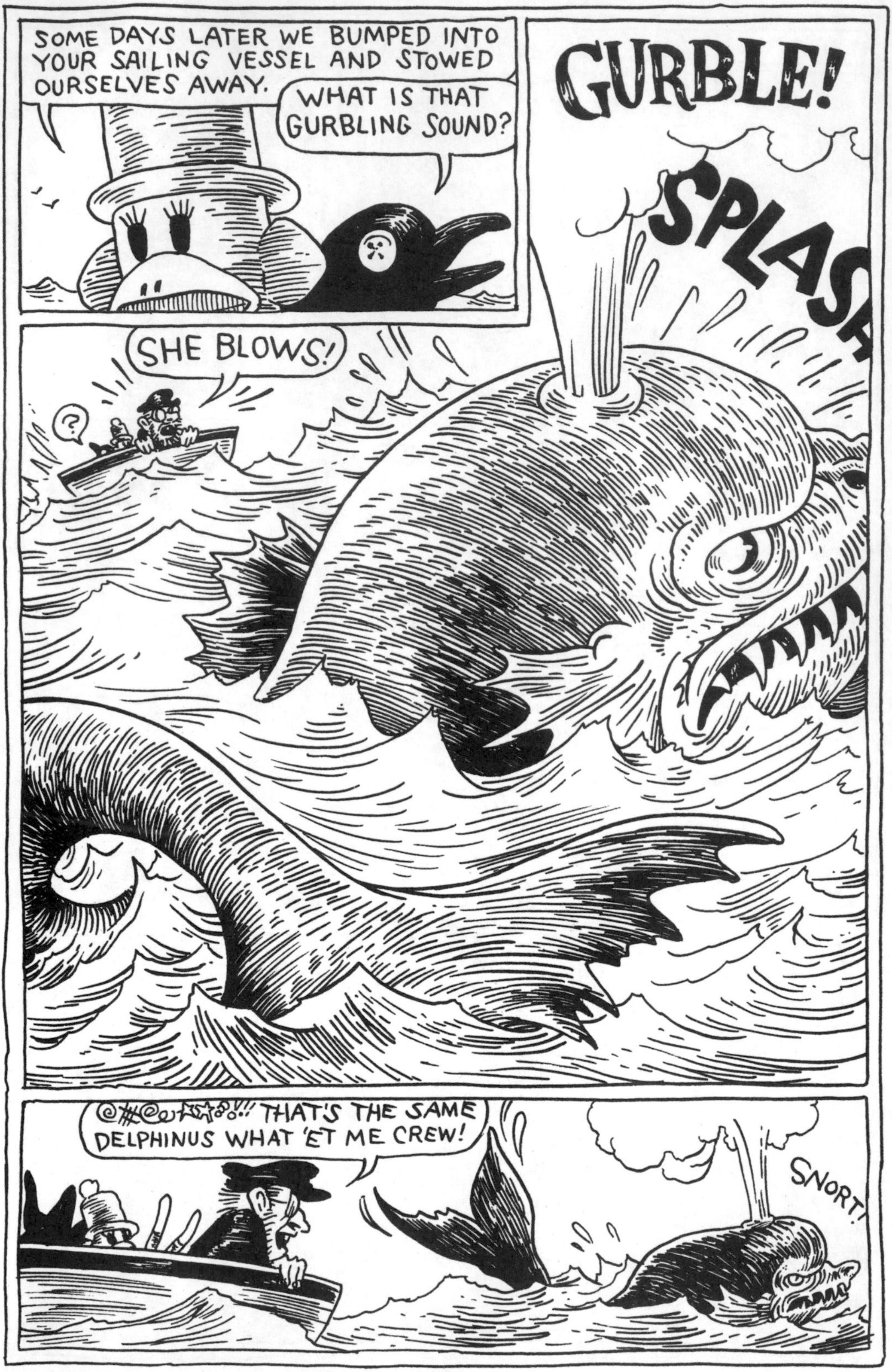
SOME DAYS LATER WE BUMPED INTO YOUR SAILING VESSEL AND STOWED OURSELVES AWAY.
WHAT IS THAT GURBLING SOUND?
GURBLE!
SPLASH
SHE BLOWS!
?
THAT'S THE SAME DELPHINUS WHAT 'ET ME CREW!
SNORT!

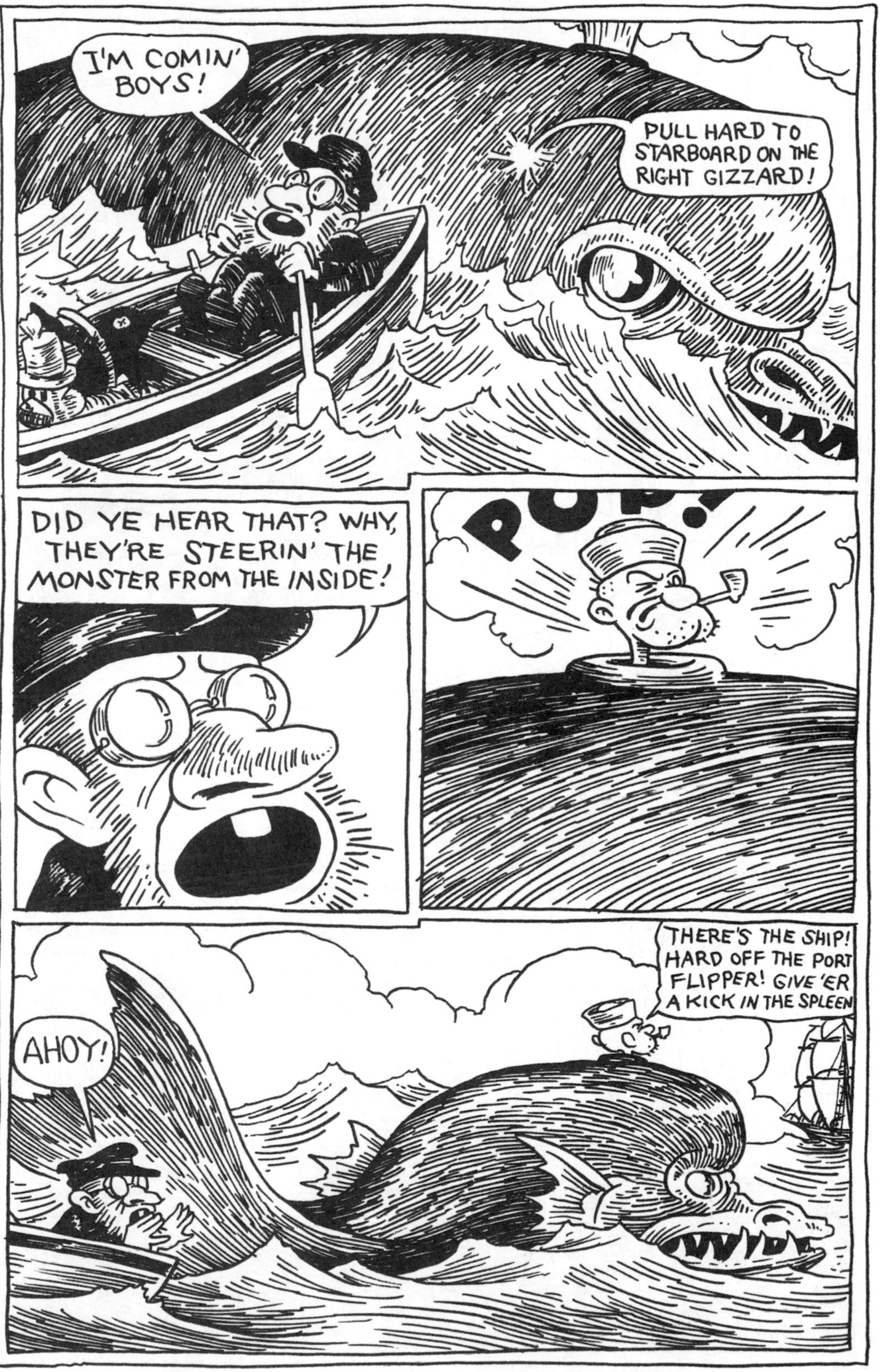
I'M COMIN' BOYS!
PULL HARD TO STARBOARD ON THE RIGHT GIZZARD!
DID YE HEAR THAT? WHY, THEY'RE STEERIN' THE MONSTER FROM THE INSIDE!
POP!
THERE'S THE SHIP! HARD OFF THE PORT FLIPPER! GIVE 'ER A KICK IN THE SPLEEN
AHOY!

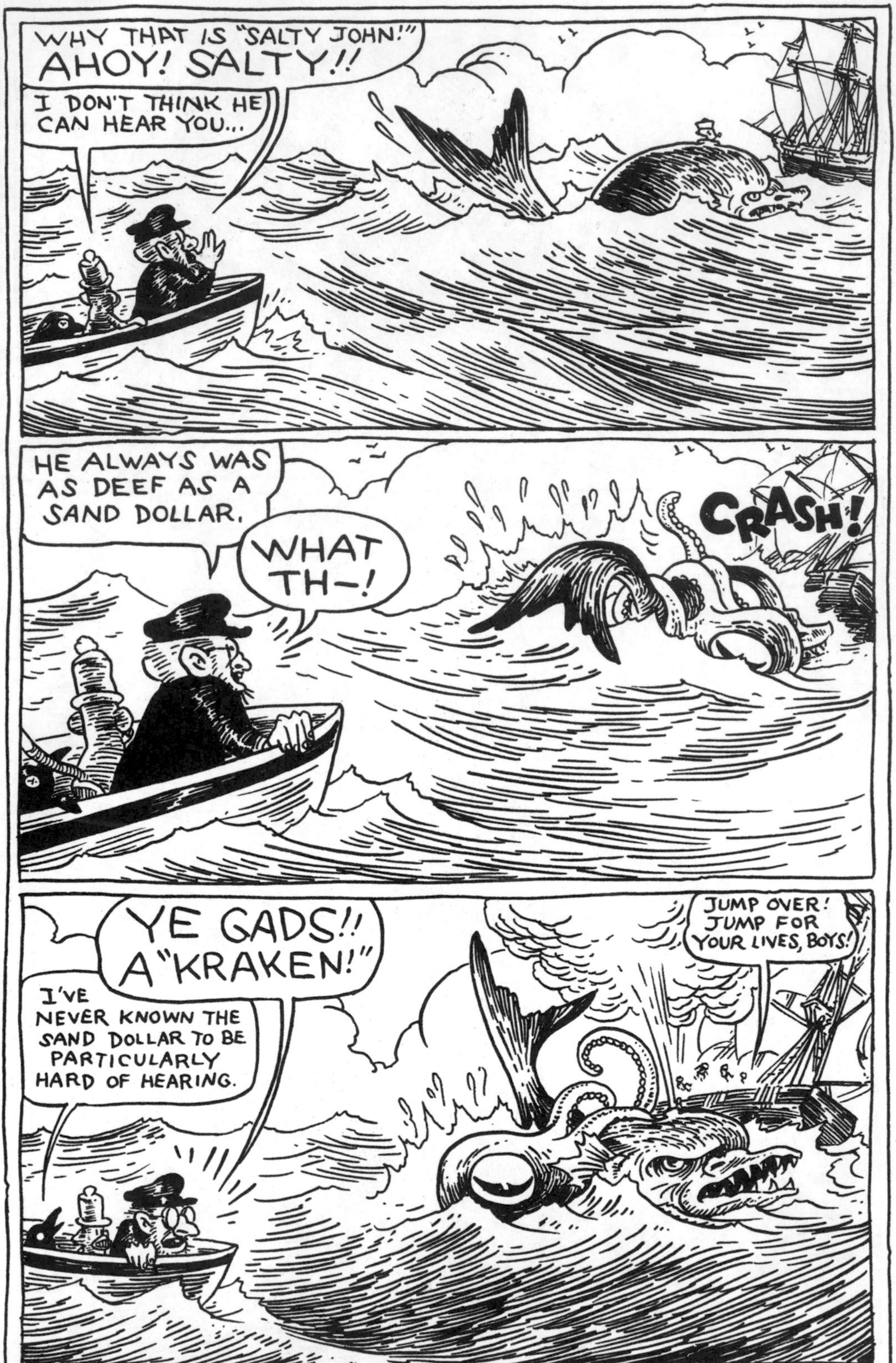
WHY THAT IS "SALTY JOHN!" AHOY! SALTY!!
I DON'T THINK HE CAN HEAR YOU...
HE ALWAYS WAS AS DEEF AS A SAND DOLLAR.
WHAT TH-!
CRASH!
YE GADS!! A "KRAKEN!"
I'VE NEVER KNOWN THE SAND DOLLAR TO BE PARTICULARLY HARD OF HEARING.
JUMP OVER! JUMP FOR YOUR LIVES, BOYS!

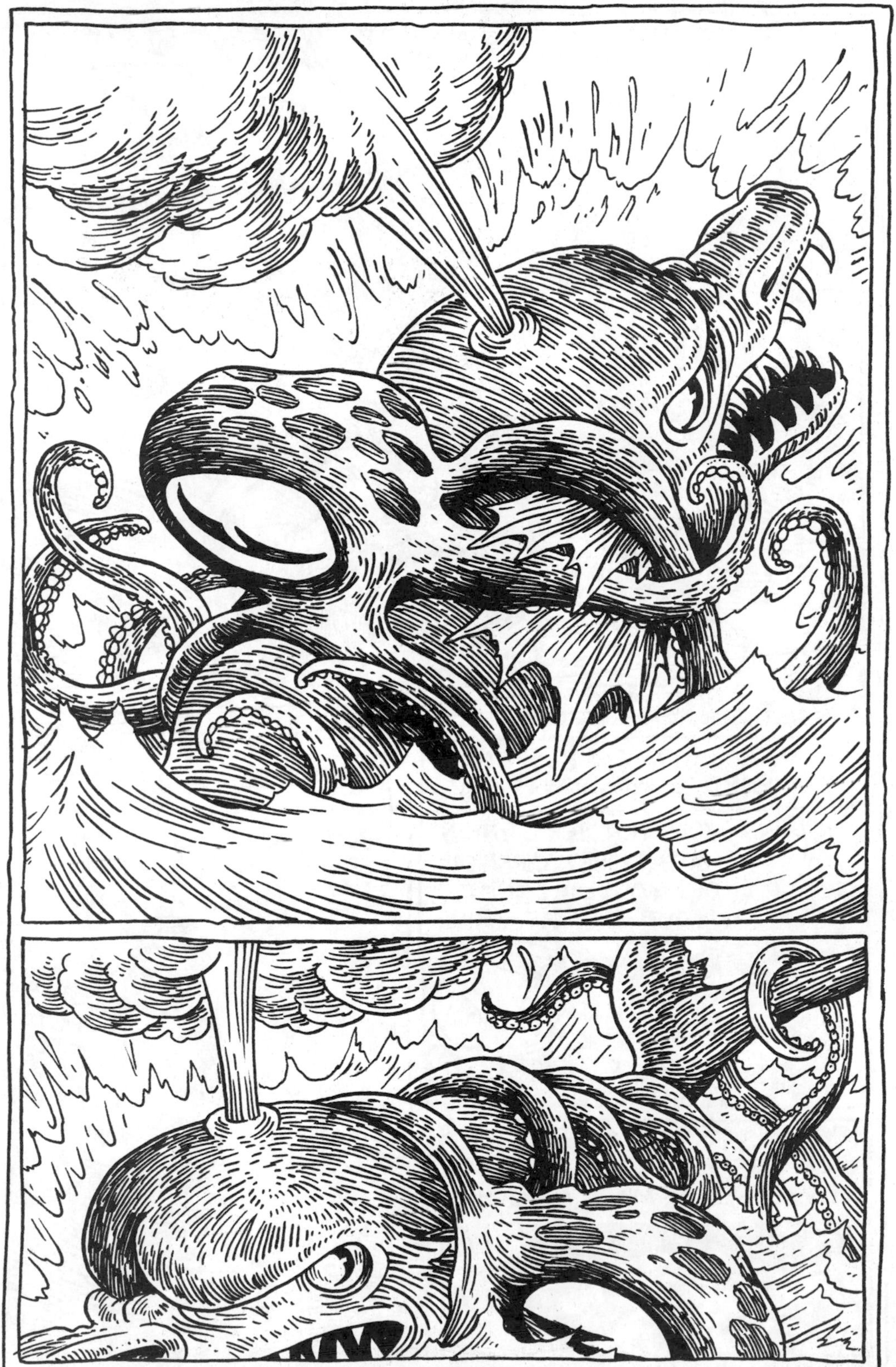

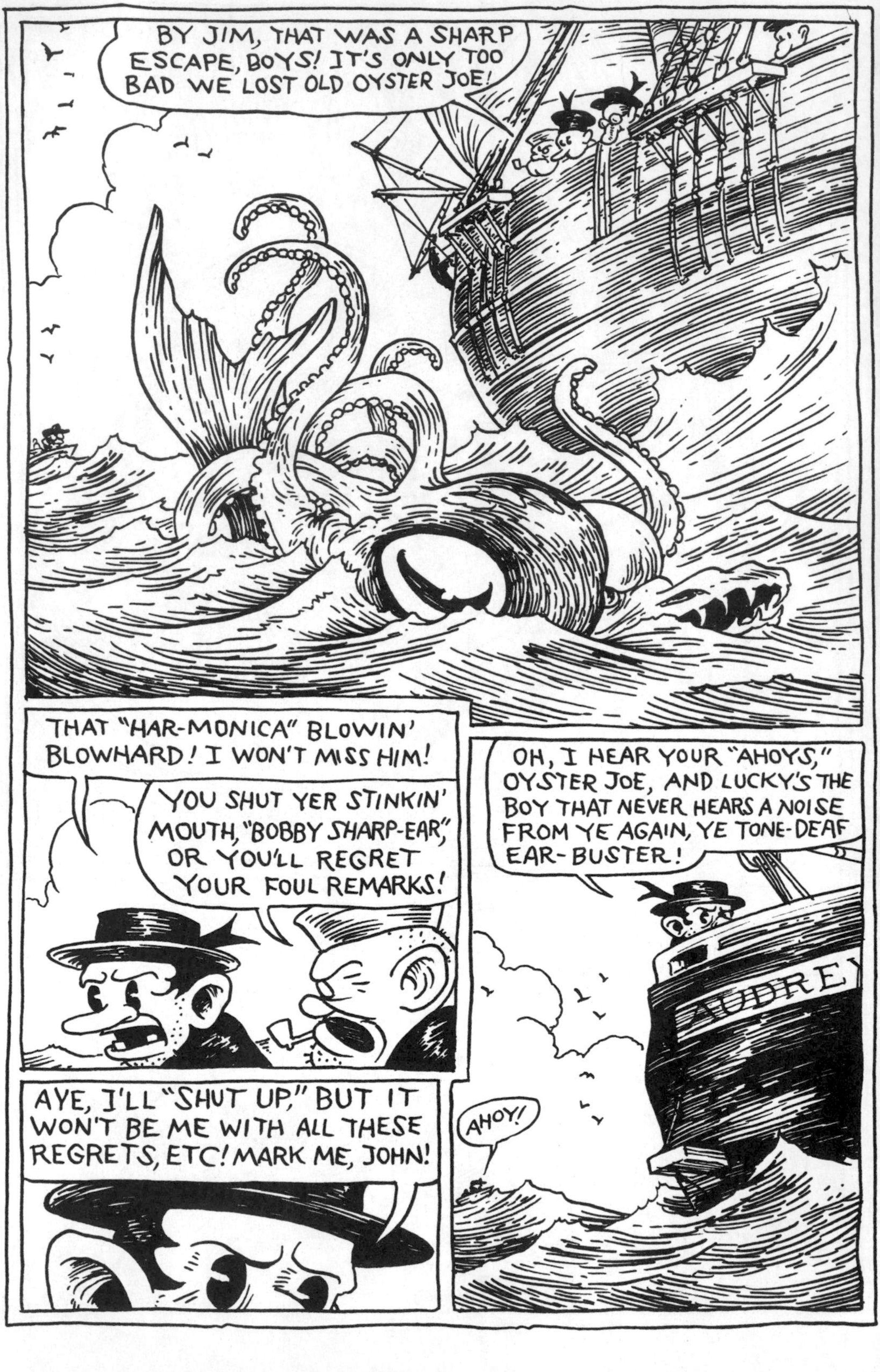
BY JIM, THAT WAS A SHARP ESCAPE, BOYS! IT'S ONLY TOO BAD WE LOST OLD OYSTER JOE!
THAT "HAR-MONICA" BLOWIN' BLOWHARD! I WON'T MISS HIM!
YOU SHUT YER STINKIN' MOUTH, "BOBBY SHARP-EAR", OR YOU'LL REGRET YOUR FOUL REMARKS!
AYE, I'LL "SHUT UP," BUT IT WON'T BE ME WITH ALL THESE REGRETS, ETC! MARK ME, JOHN!
OH, I HEAR YOUR "AHOYS," OYSTER JOE, AND LUCKY'S THE BOY THAT NEVER HEARS A NOISE FROM YE AGAIN, YE TONE-DEAF EAR-BUSTER!
AUDREY
AHOY!

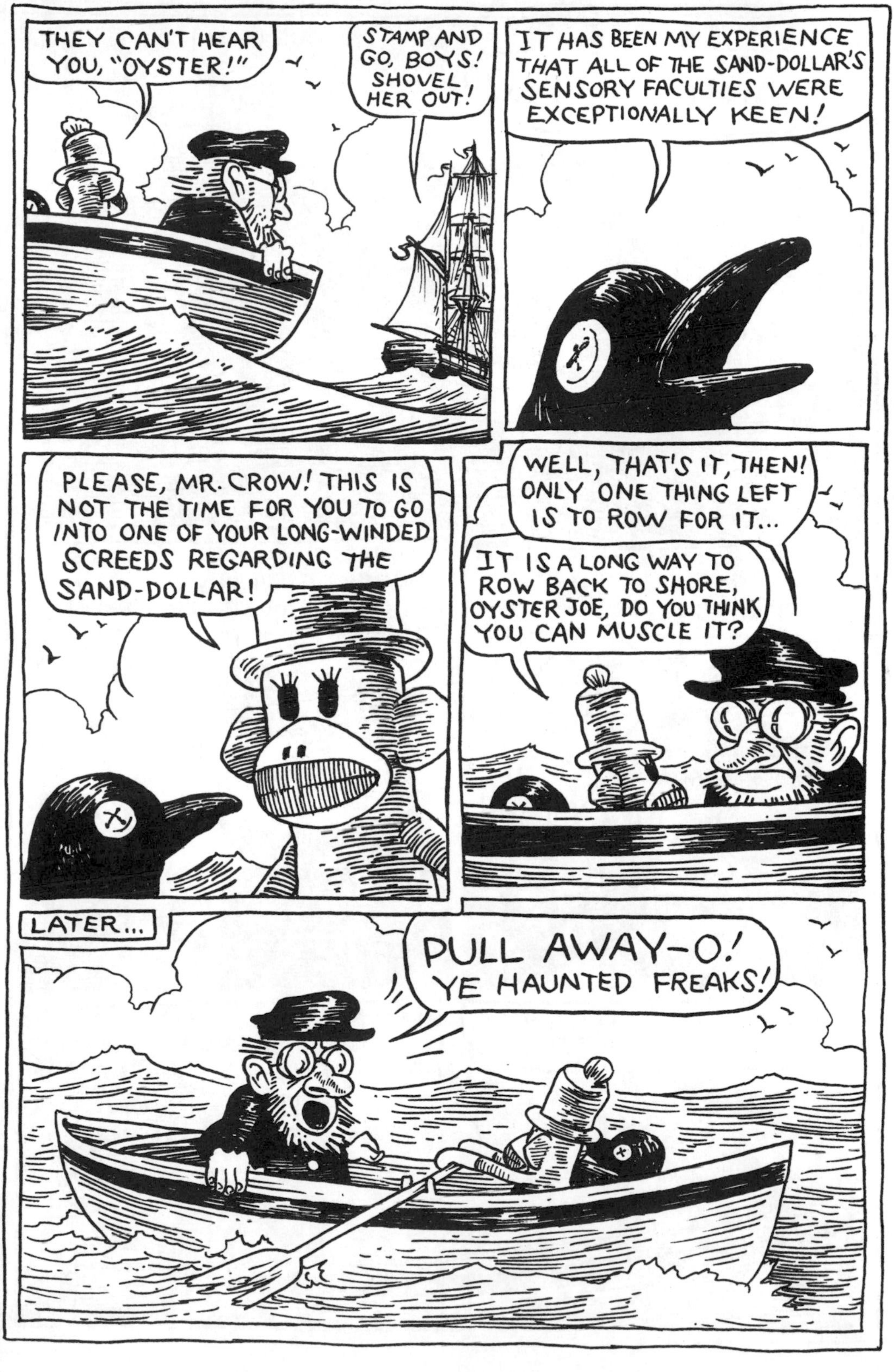
THEY CAN'T HEAR YOU, "OYSTER!"
STAMP AND GO, BOYS! SHOVEL HER OUT!
IT HAS BEEN MY EXPERIENCE THAT ALL OF THE SAND-DOLLAR'S SENSORY FACULTIES WERE EXCEPTIONALLY KEEN!
PLEASE, MR. CROW! THIS IS NOT THE TIME FOR YOU TO GO INTO ONE OF YOUR LONG-WINDED SCREEDS REGARDING THE SAND-DOLLAR!
WELL, THAT'S IT, THEN! ONLY ONE THING LEFT IS TO ROW FOR IT...
IT IS A LONG WAY TO ROW BACK TO SHORE, OYSTER JOE, DO YOU THINK YOU CAN MUSCLE IT?
LATER...
PULL AWAY-O! YE HAUNTED FREAKS!

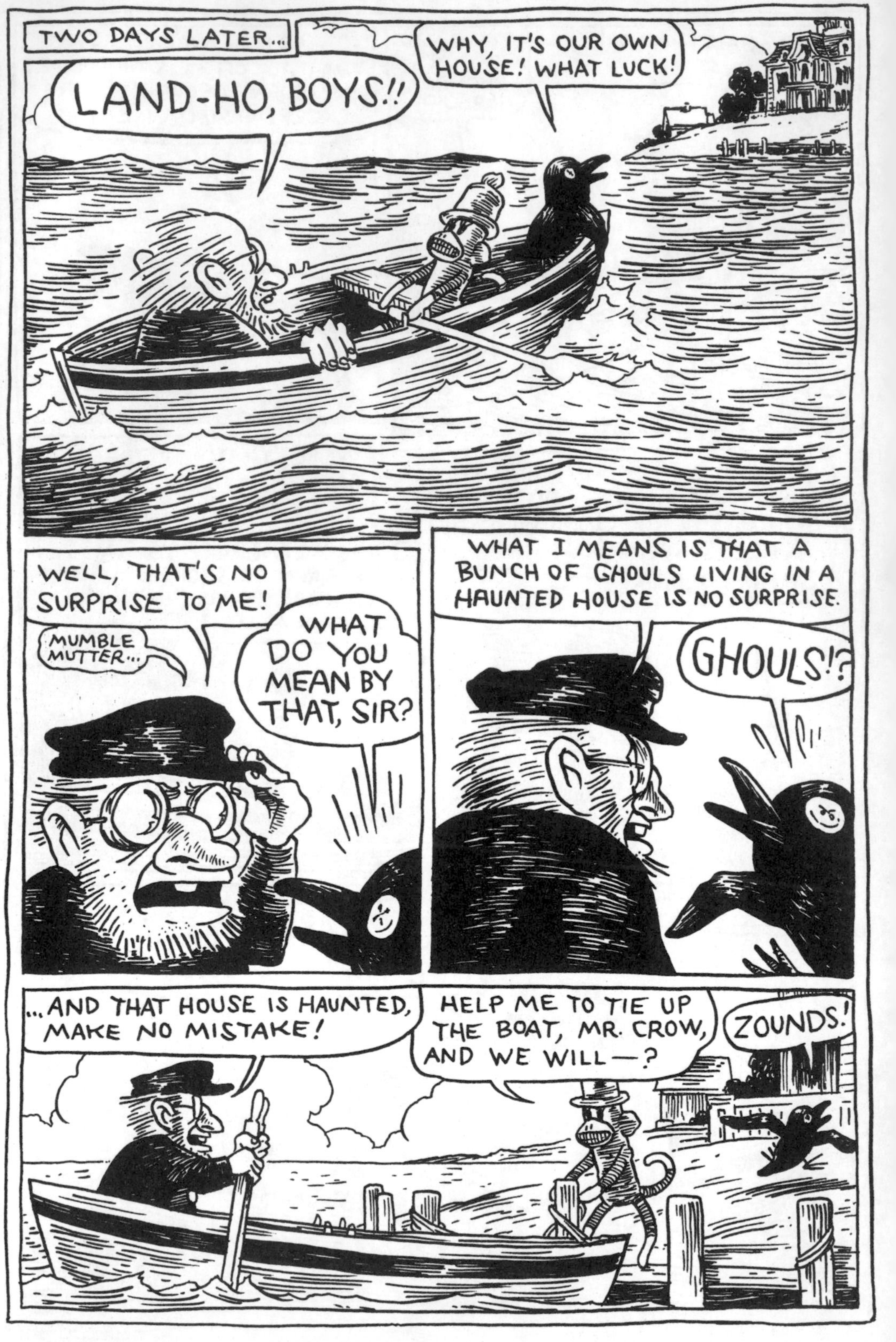
TWO DAYS LATER...
LAND-HO, BOYS!!
WHY, IT'S OUR OWN HOUSE! WHAT LUCK!
WELL, THAT'S NO SURPRISE TO ME!
MUMBLE MUTTER...
WHAT DO YOU MEAN BY THAT, SIR?
WHAT I MEANS IS THAT A BUNCH OF GHOULS LIVING IN A HAUNTED HOUSE IS NO SURPRISE.
GHOULS!?
...AND THAT HOUSE IS HAUNTED, MAKE NO MISTAKE!
HELP ME TO TIE UP THE BOAT, MR. CROW, AND WE WILL—?
ZOUNDS!

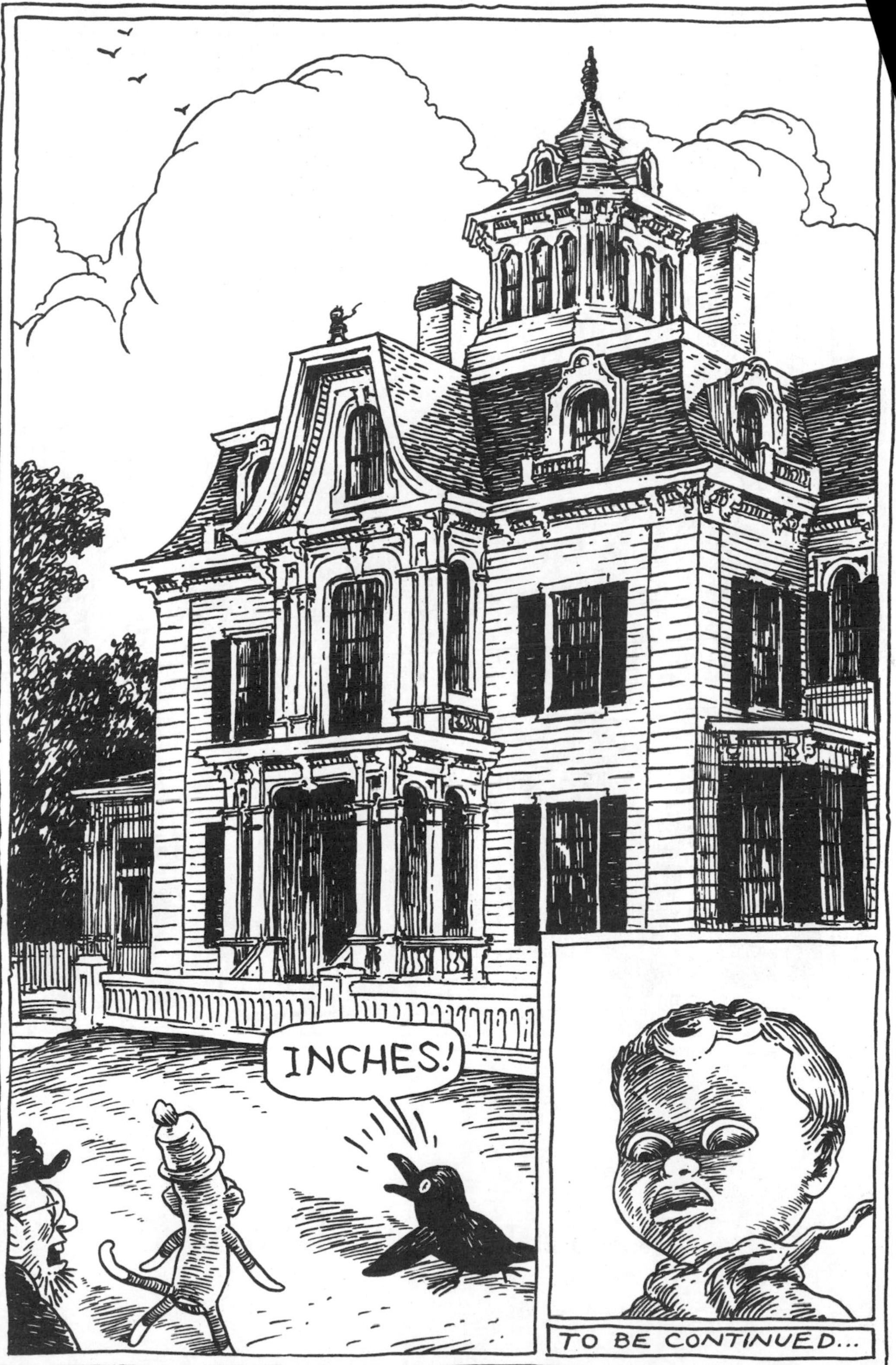
INCHES!
TO BE CONTINUED...

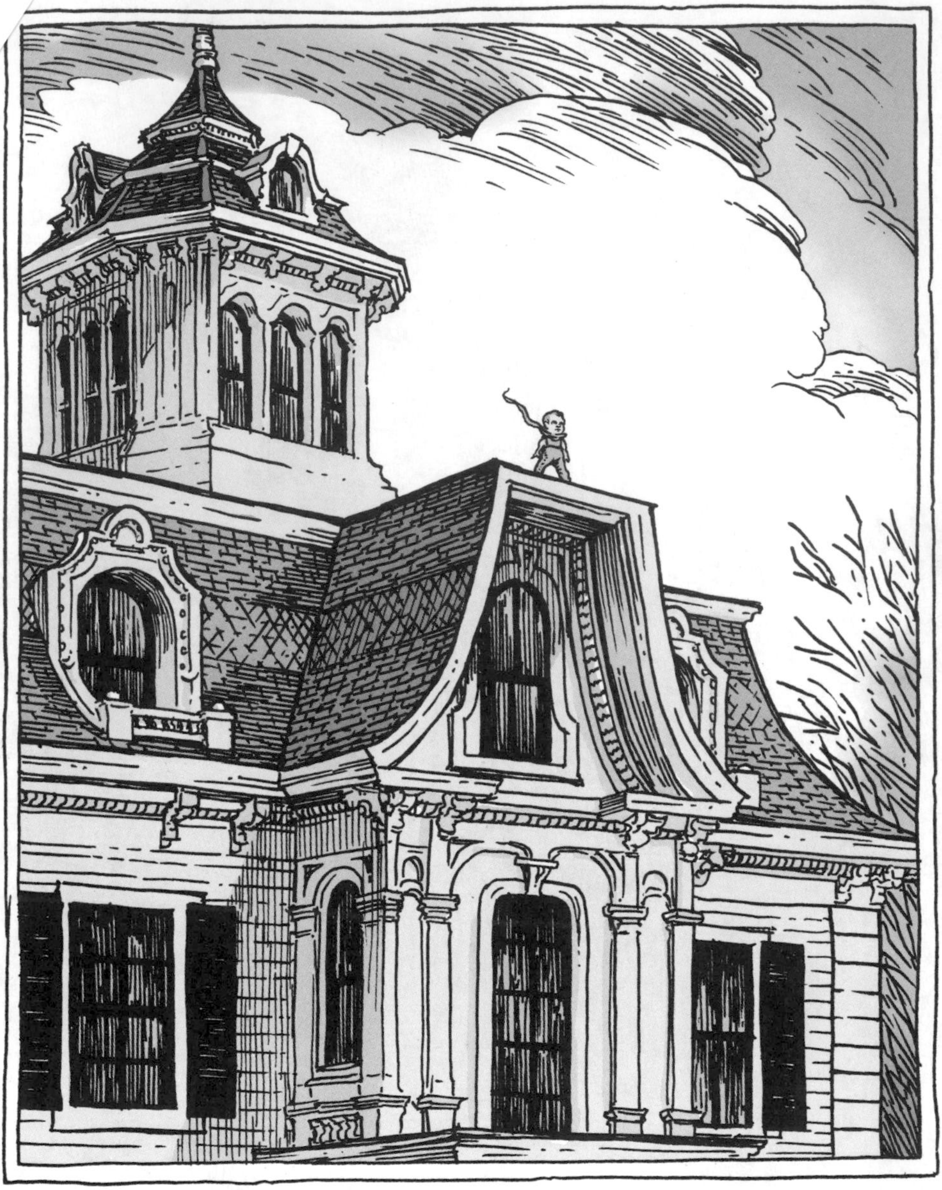

Chapter Two

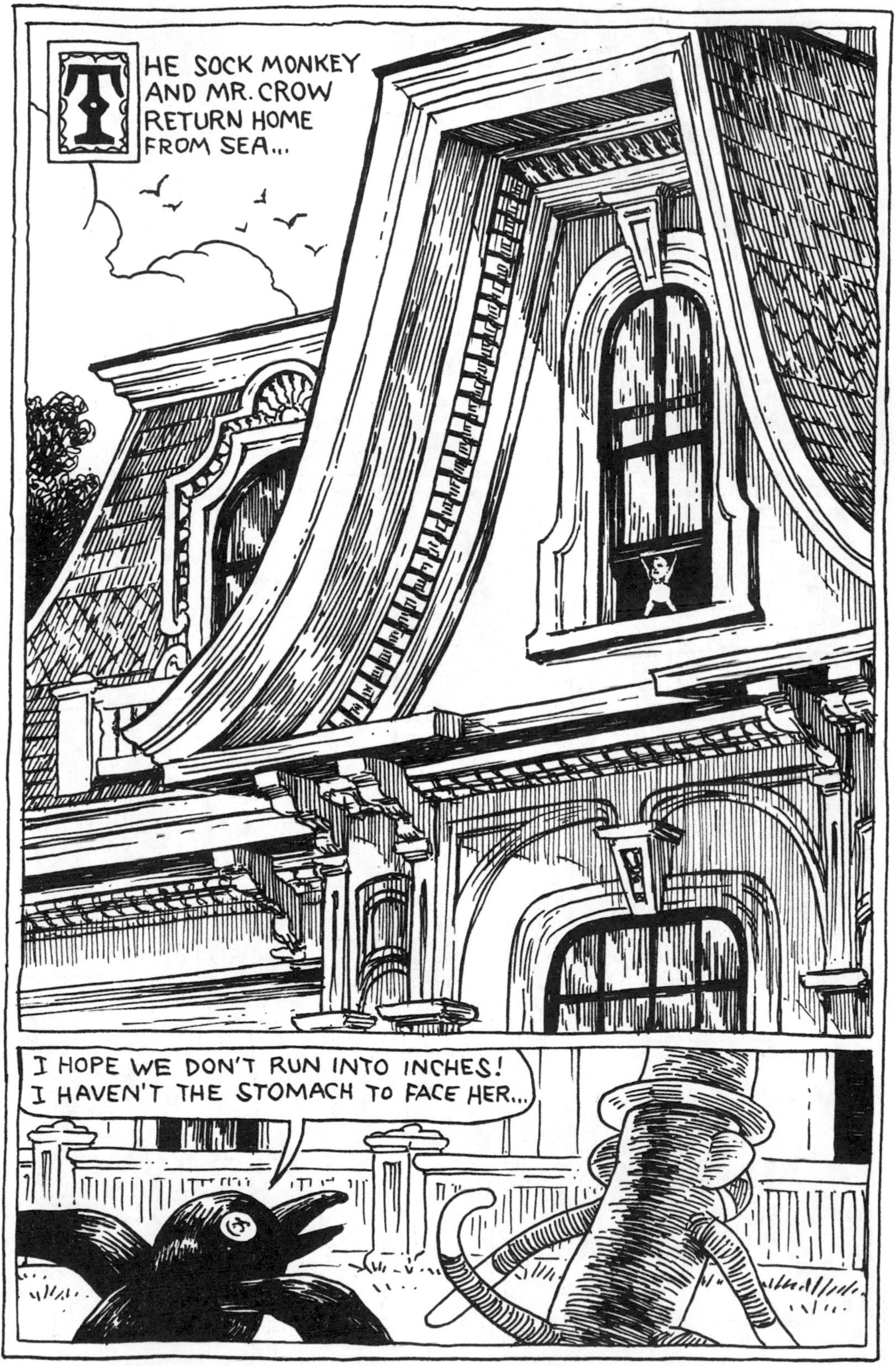
THE SOCK MONKEY AND MR. CROW RETURN HOME FROM SEA...
I HOPE WE DON'T RUN INTO INCHES! I HAVEN'T THE STOMACH TO FACE HER...

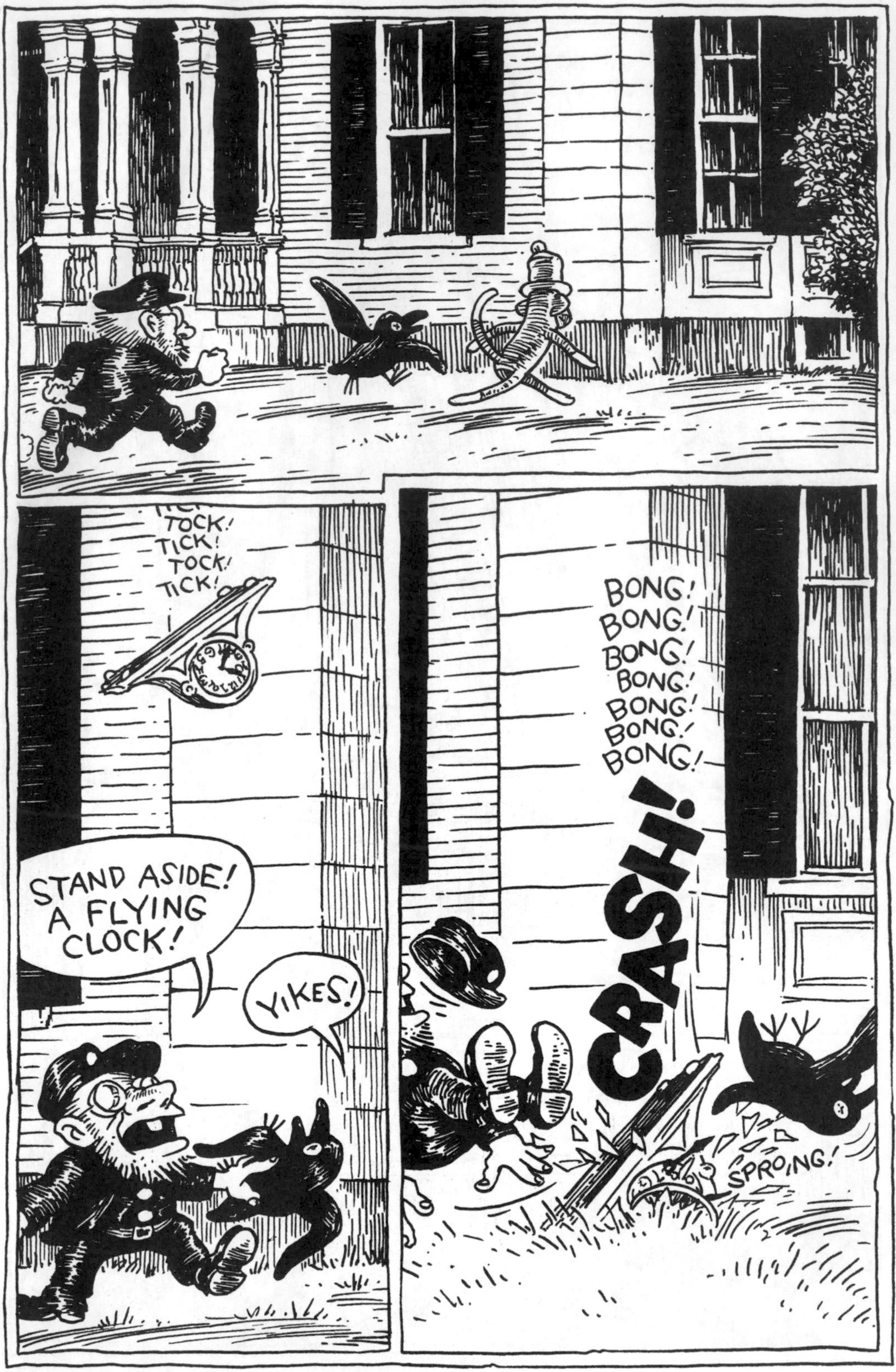
TOCK!
TICK!
TOCK!
TICK!
STAND ASIDE! A FLYING CLOCK!
YIKES!
BONG!
BONG!
BONG!
BONG!
BONG!
BONG!
BONG!
CRASH!
SPROING!

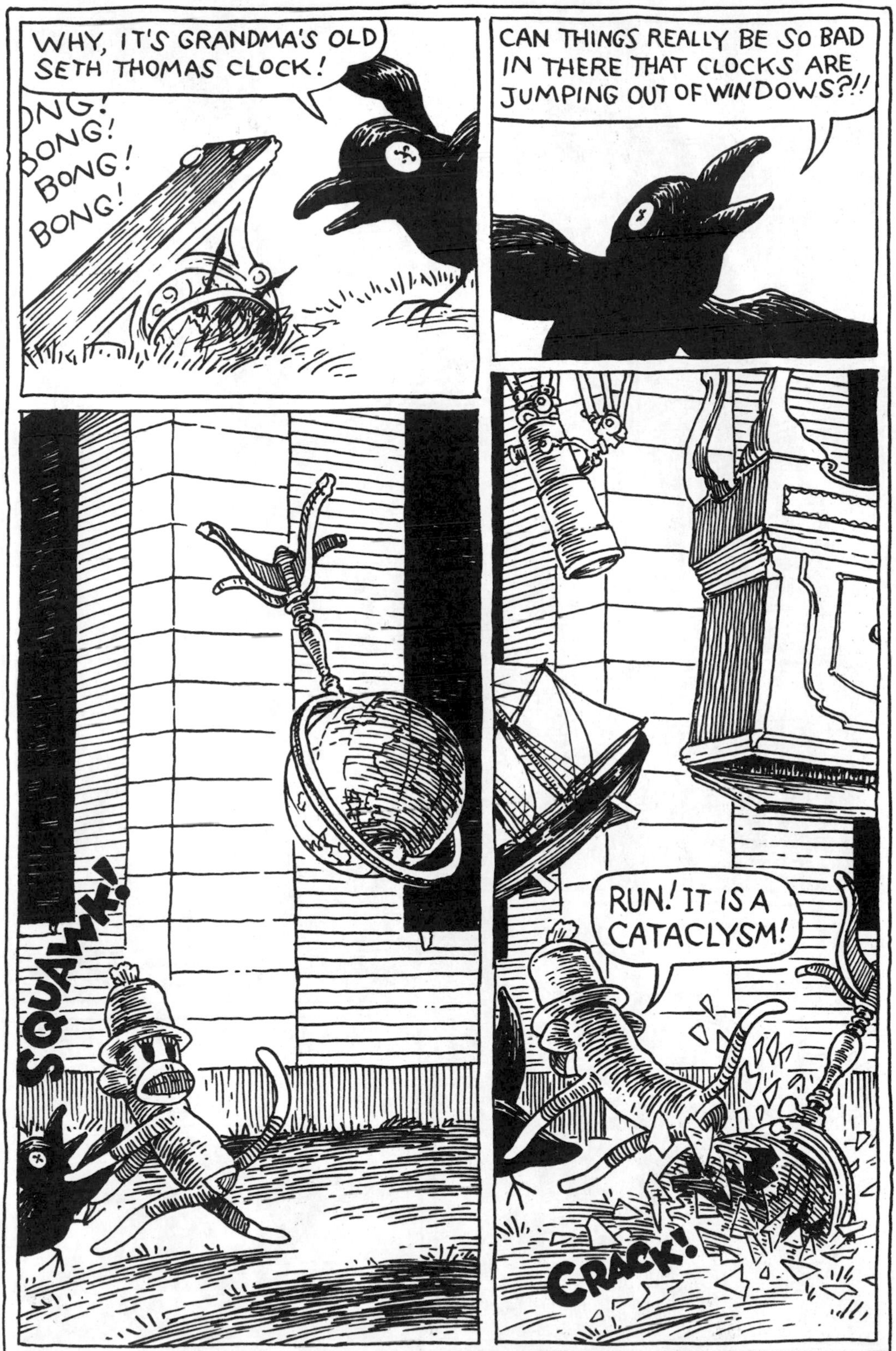
WHY, IT'S GRANDMA'S OLD SETH THOMAS CLOCK!
ONG! BONG! BONG! BONG!
CAN THINGS REALLY BE SO BAD IN THERE THAT CLOCKS ARE JUMPING OUT OF WINDOWS?!!
SQUAWK!
RUN! IT IS A CATACLYSM!
CRACK!

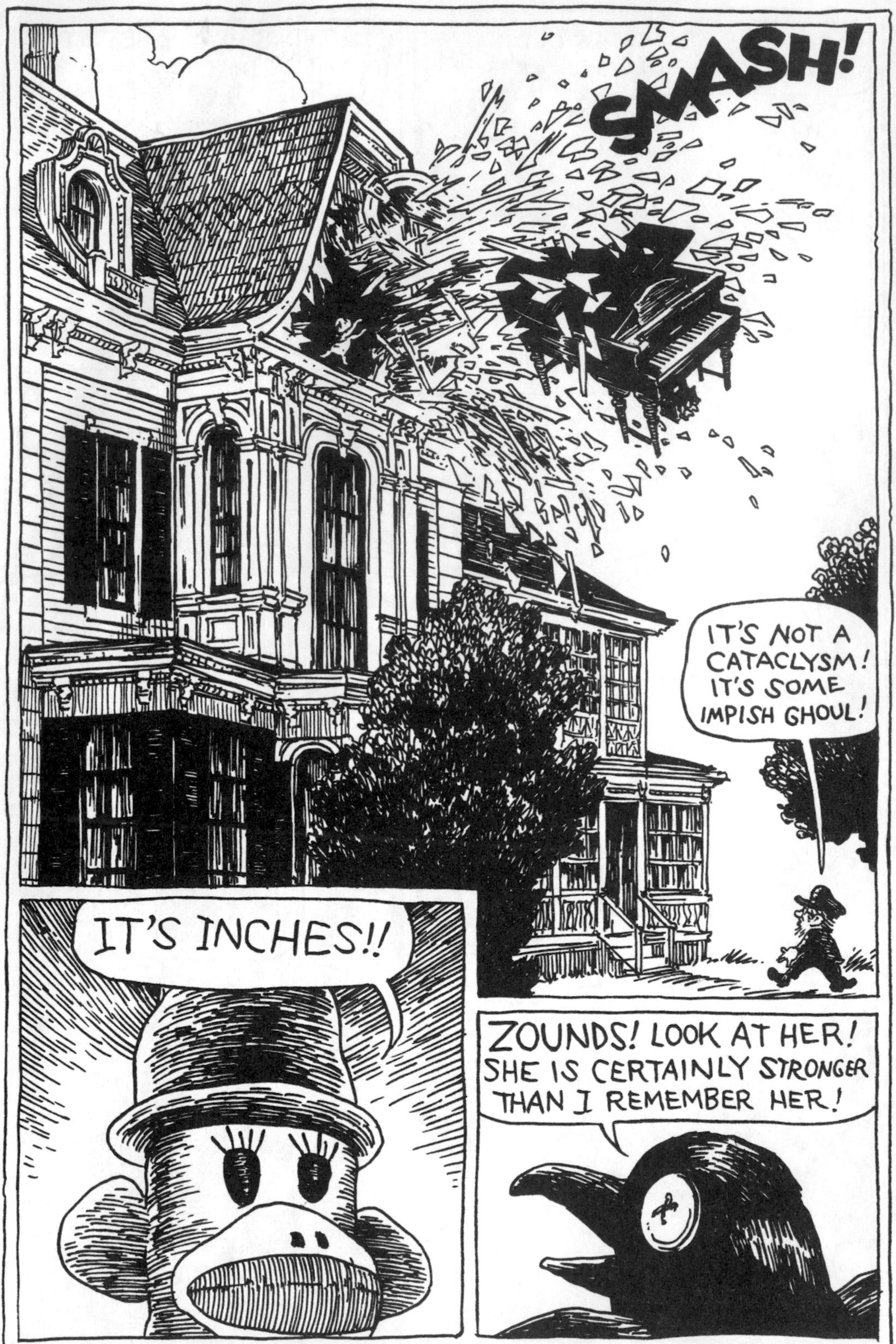
SMASH!
IT'S NOT A CATACLYSM! IT'S SOME IMPISH GHOUL!
IT'S INCHES!!
ZOUNDS! LOOK AT HER! SHE IS CERTAINLY STRONGER THAN I REMEMBER HER!

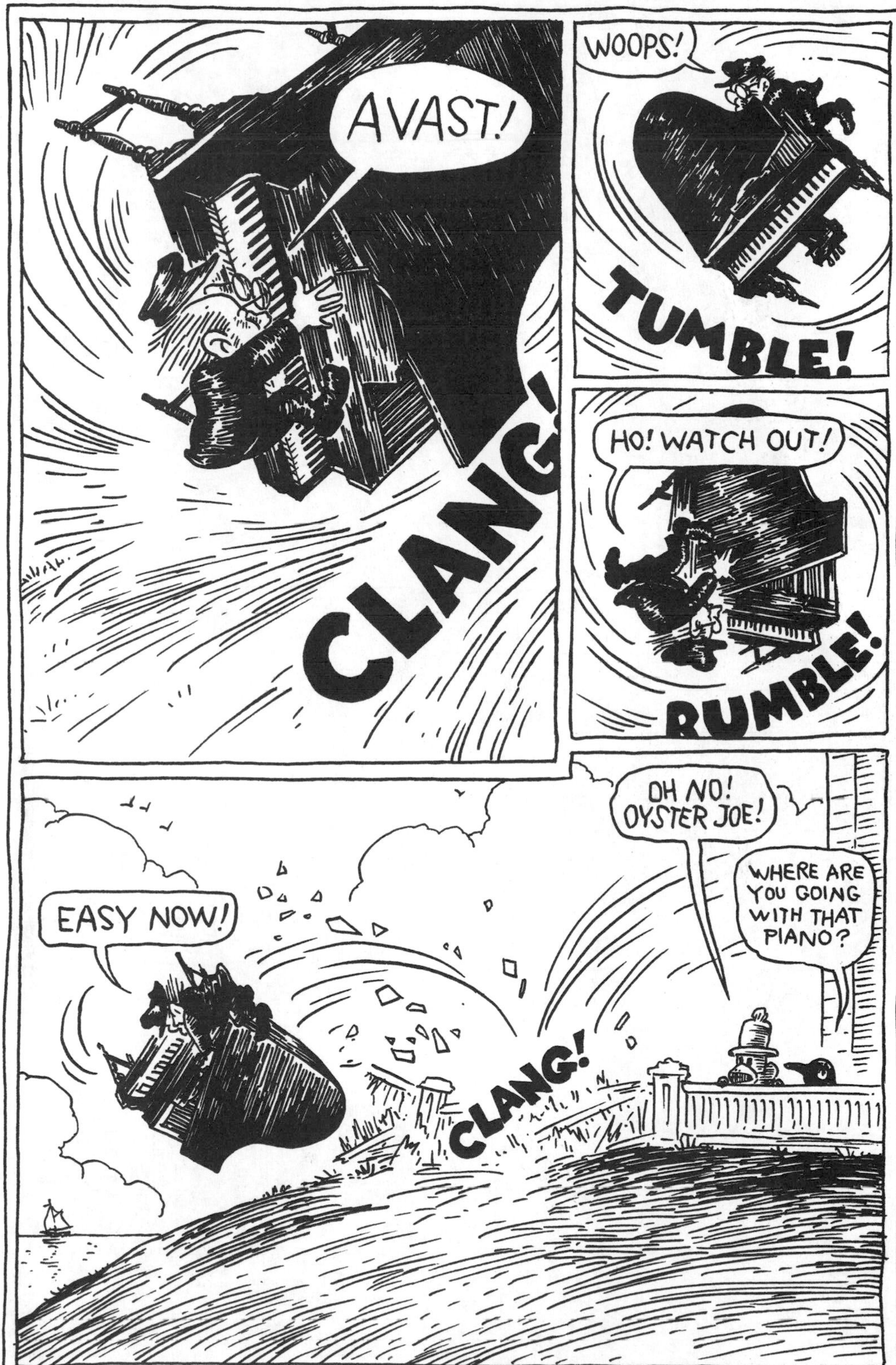
AVAST!
CLANG!
WOOPS!
TUMBLE!
HO! WATCH OUT!
RUMBLE!
EASY NOW!
CLANG!
OH NO! OYSTER JOE!
WHERE ARE YOU GOING WITH THAT PIANO?

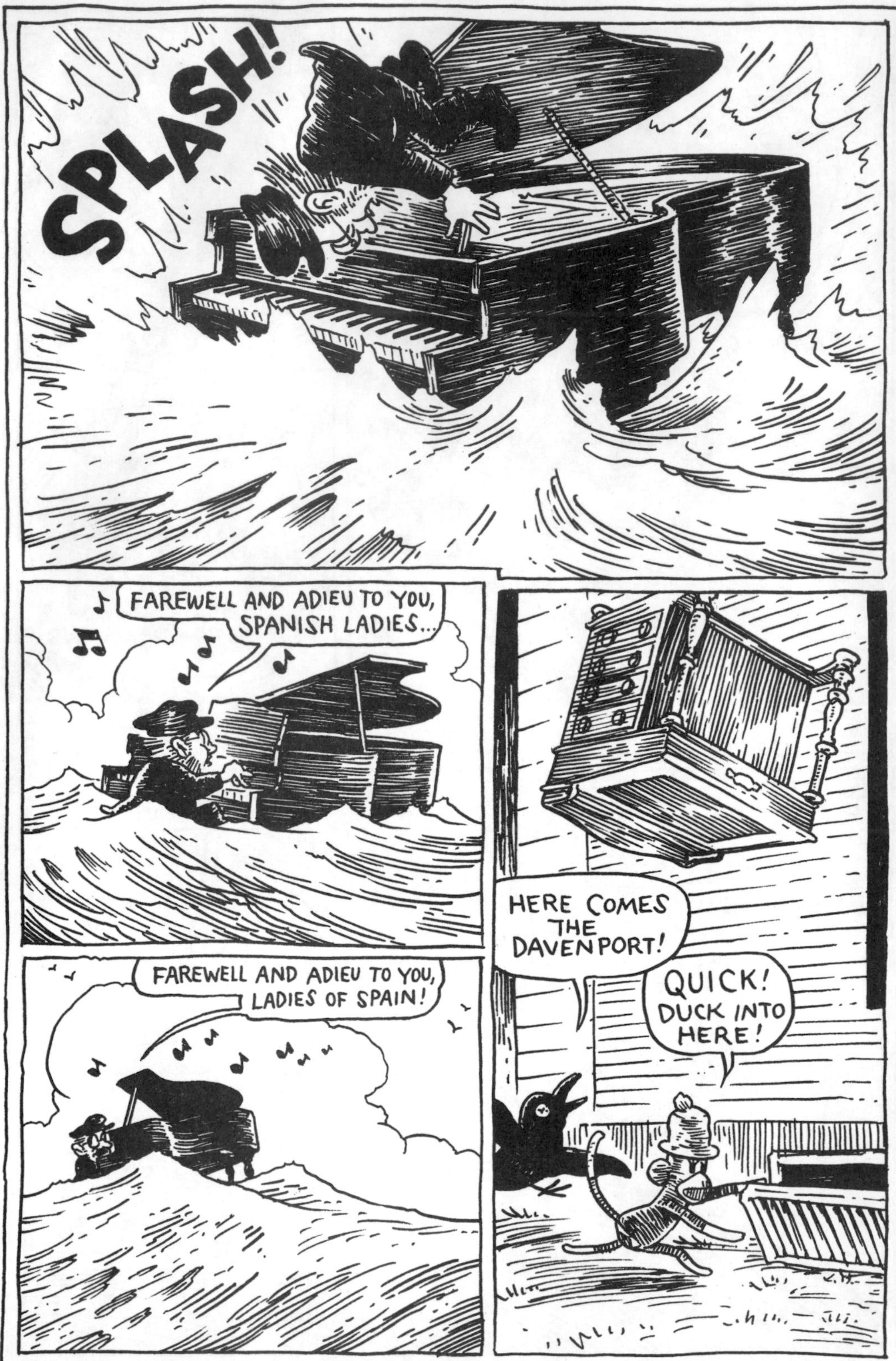
SPLASH!
FAREWELL AND ADIEU TO YOU, SPANISH LADIES...
HERE COMES THE DAVENPORT!
QUICK! DUCK INTO HERE!
FAREWELL AND ADIEU TO YOU, LADIES OF SPAIN!

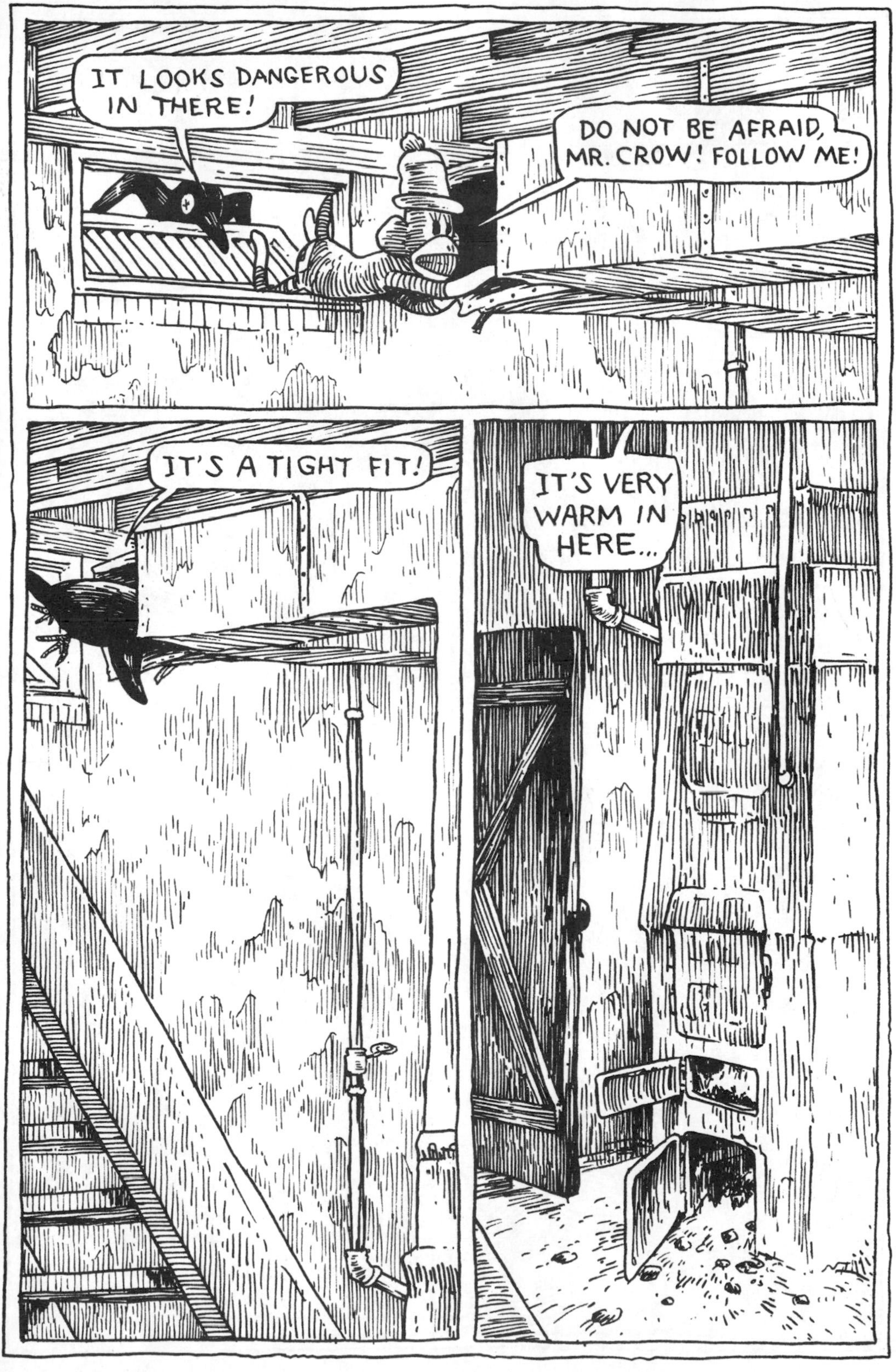
IT LOOKS DANGEROUS IN THERE!
DO NOT BE AFRAID, MR. CROW! FOLLOW ME!
IT'S A TIGHT FIT!
IT'S VERY WARM IN HERE...

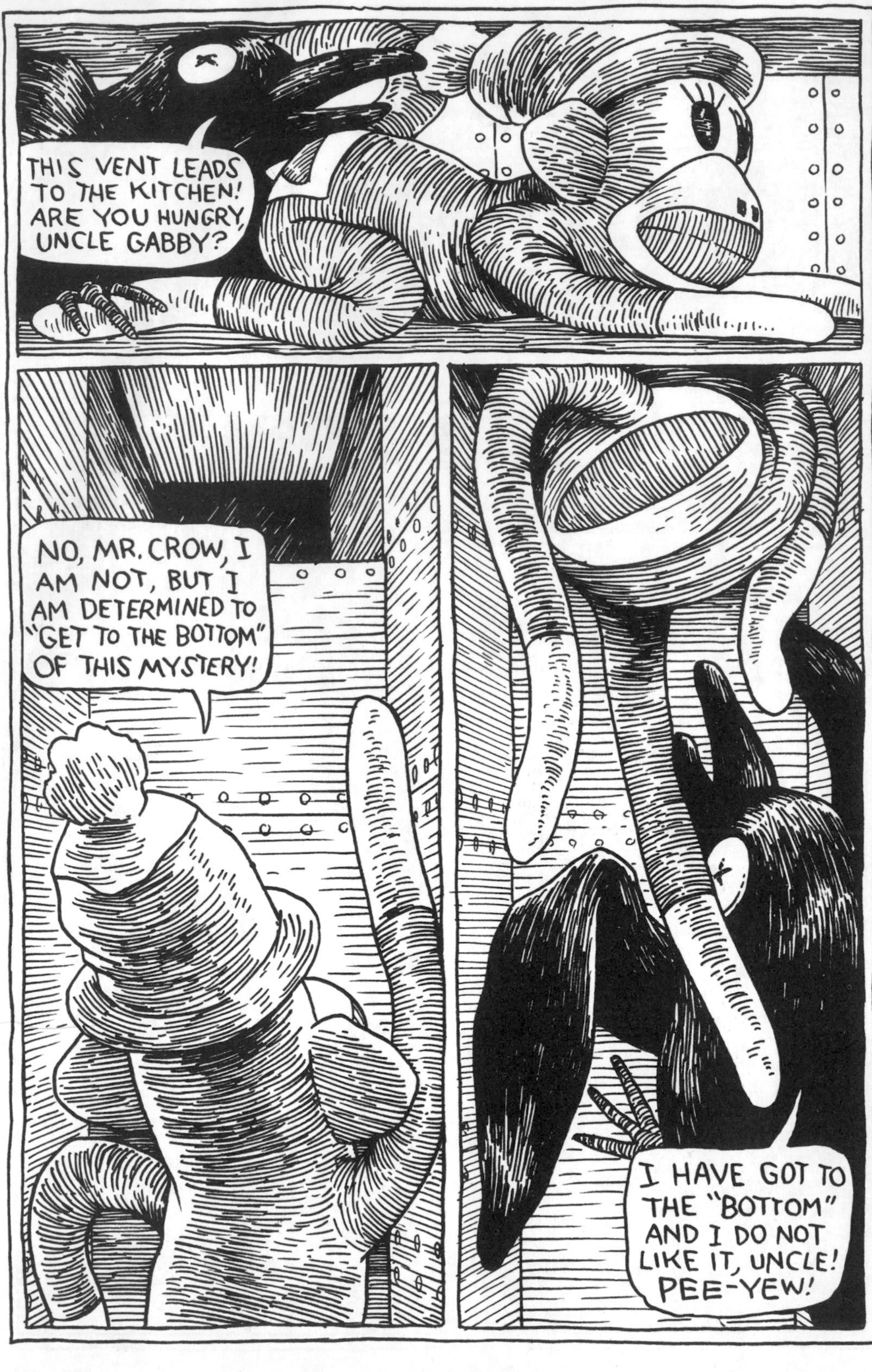
THIS VENT LEADS TO THE KITCHEN! ARE YOU HUNGRY UNCLE GABBY?
NO, MR. CROW, I AM NOT, BUT I AM DETERMINED TO "GET TO THE BOTTOM" OF THIS MYSTERY!
I HAVE GOT TO THE "BOTTOM" AND I DO NOT LIKE IT, UNCLE! PEE-YEW!

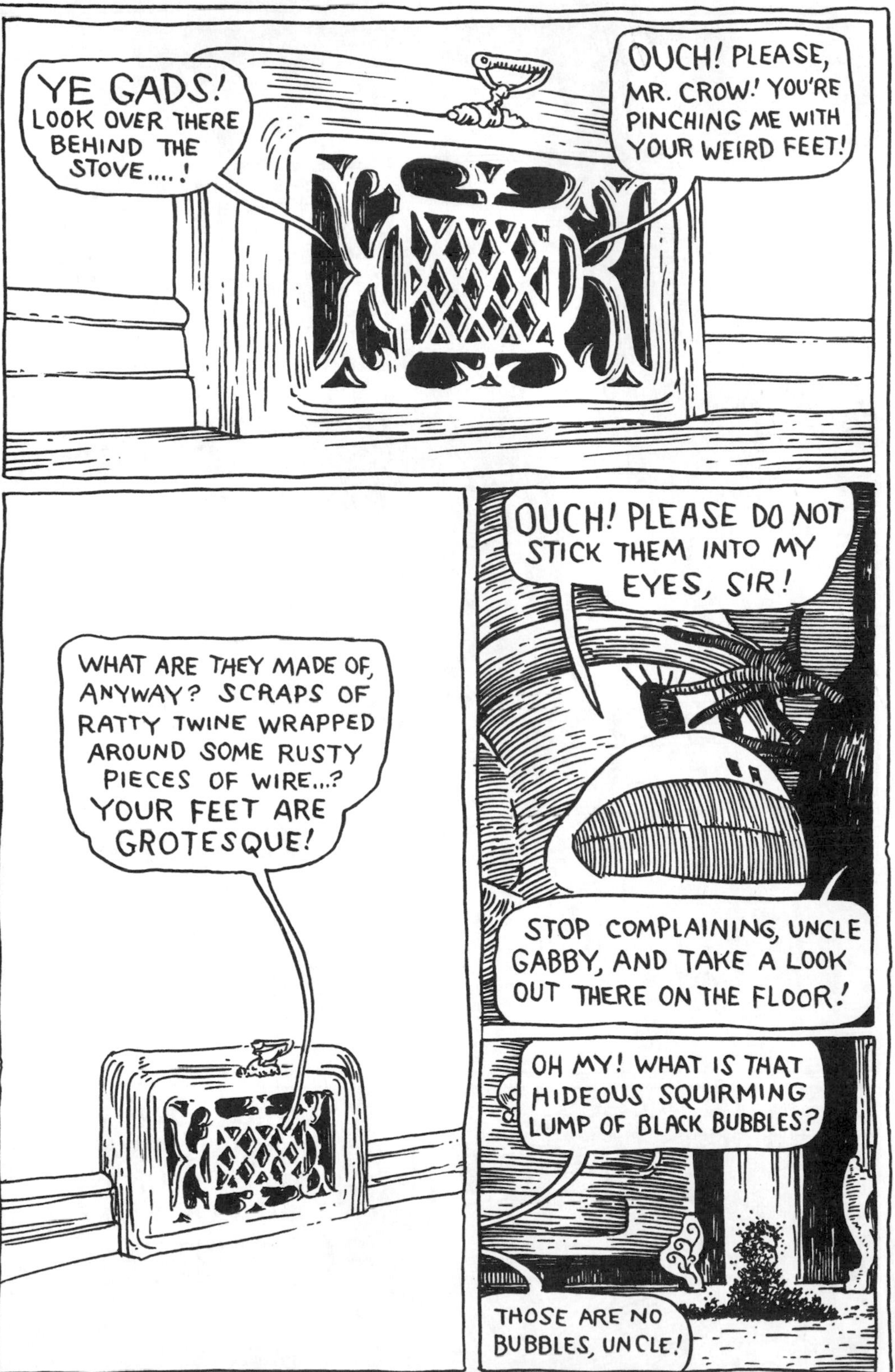
YE GADS! LOOK OVER THERE BEHIND THE STOVE....!
OUCH! PLEASE, MR. CROW! YOU'RE PINCHING ME WITH YOUR WEIRD FEET!
WHAT ARE THEY MADE OF, ANYWAY? SCRAPS OF RATTY TWINE WRAPPED AROUND SOME RUSTY PIECES OF WIRE...? YOUR FEET ARE GROTESQUE!
OUCH! PLEASE DO NOT STICK THEM INTO MY EYES, SIR!
STOP COMPLAINING, UNCLE GABBY, AND TAKE A LOOK OUT THERE ON THE FLOOR!
OH MY! WHAT IS THAT HIDEOUS SQUIRMING LUMP OF BLACK BUBBLES?
THOSE ARE NO BUBBLES, UNCLE!

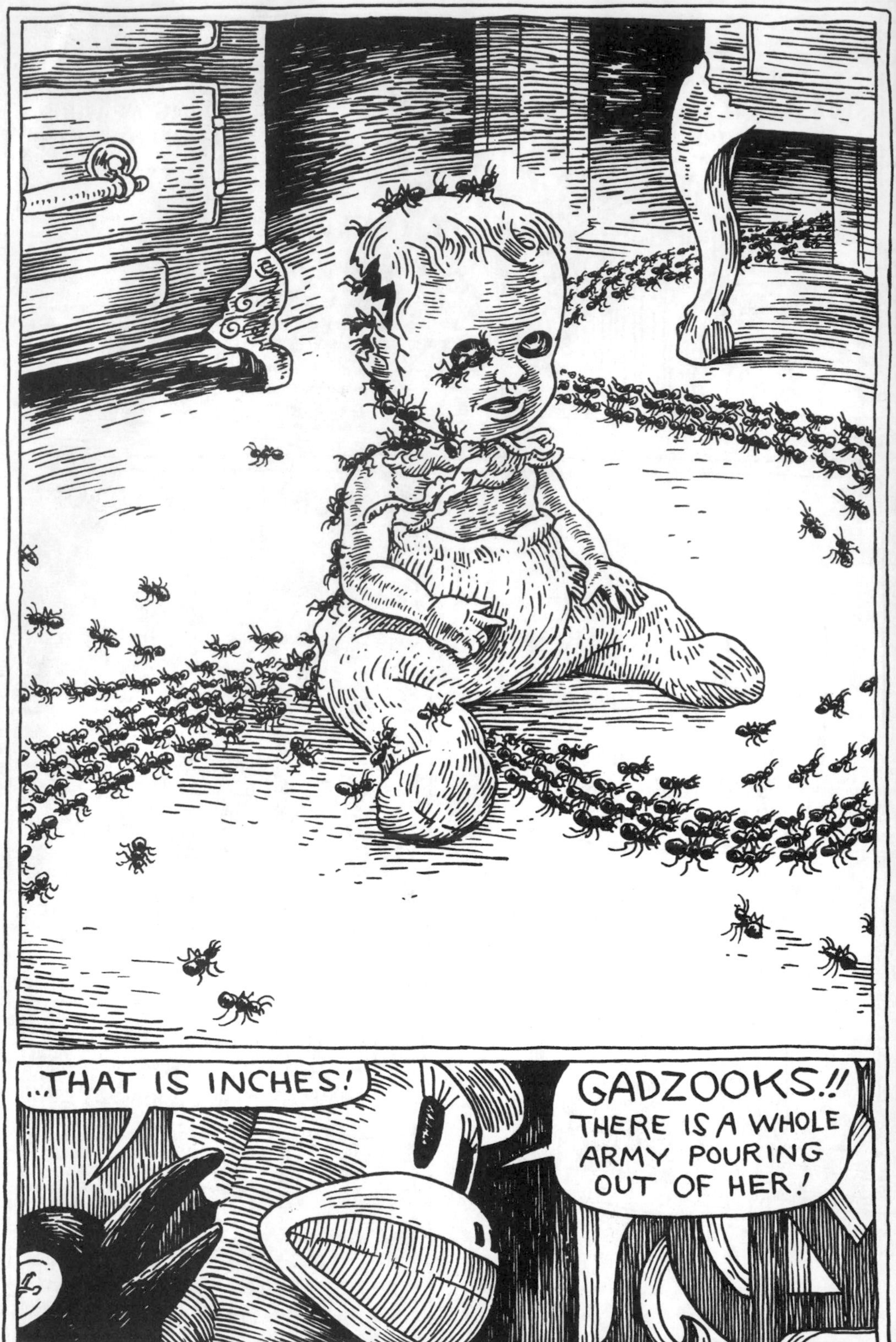
..THAT IS INCHES!
GADZOOKS!!
THERE IS A WHOLE ARMY POURING OUT OF HER!

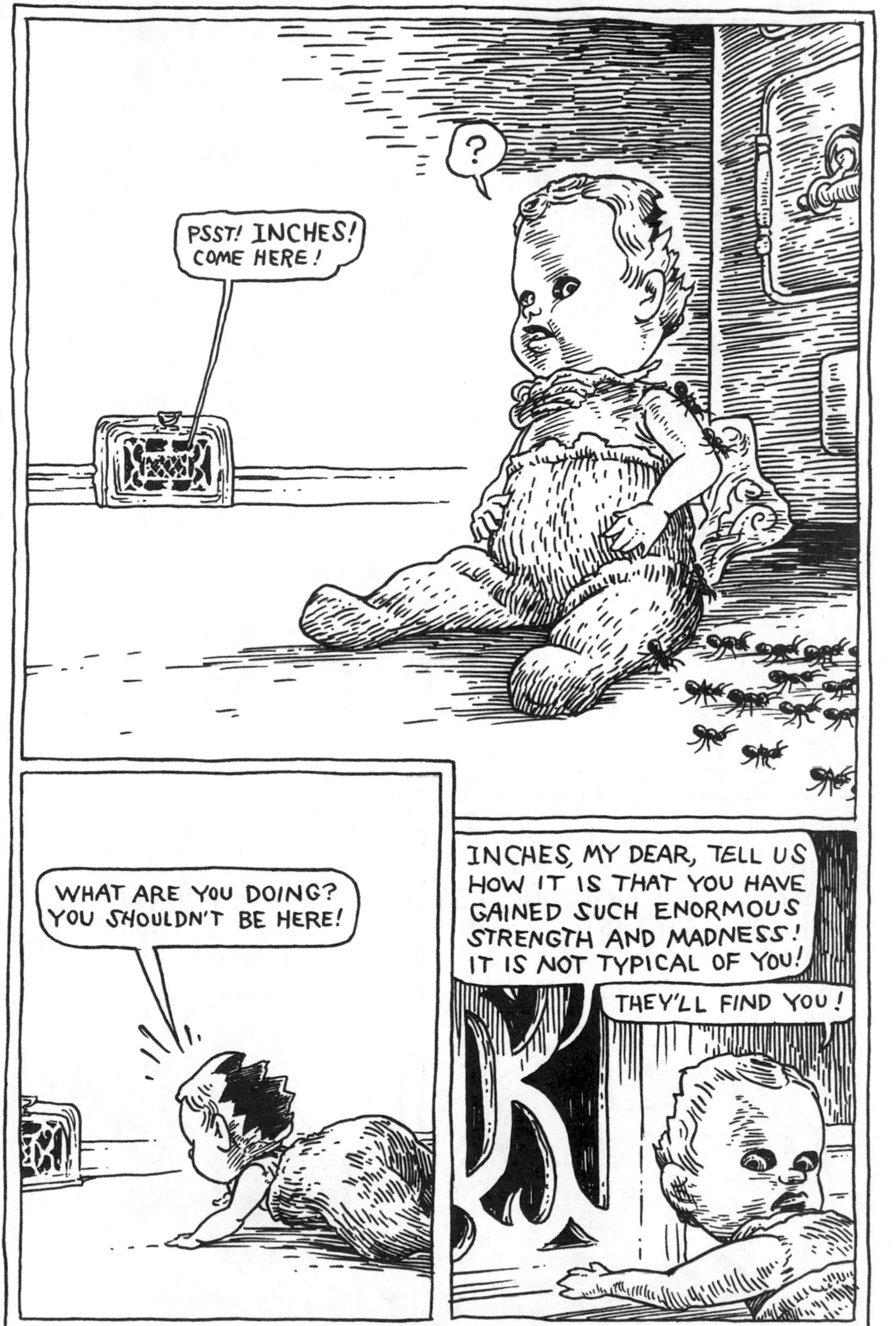
?
PSST! INCHES! COME HERE!
WHAT ARE YOU DOING? YOU SHOULDN'T BE HERE!
INCHES, MY DEAR, TELL US HOW IT IS THAT YOU HAVE GAINED SUCH ENORMOUS STRENGTH AND MADNESS! IT IS NOT TYPICAL OF YOU!
THEY'LL FIND YOU!

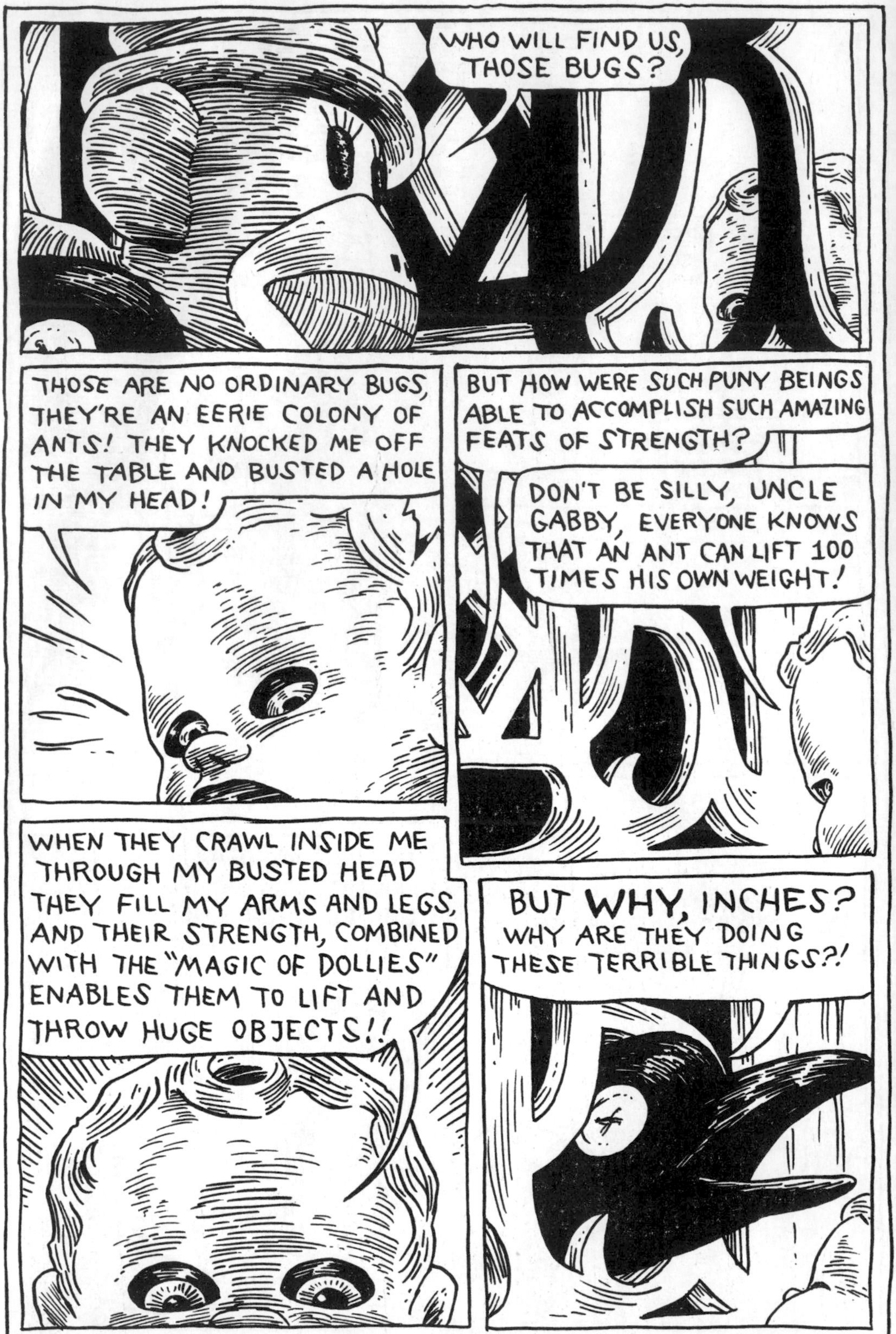
WHO WILL FIND US, THOSE BUGS?
THOSE ARE NO ORDINARY BUGS, THEY'RE AN EERIE COLONY OF ANTS! THEY KNOCKED ME OFF THE TABLE AND BUSTED A HOLE IN MY HEAD!
BUT HOW WERE SUCH PUNY BEINGS ABLE TO ACCOMPLISH SUCH AMAZING FEATS OF STRENGTH?
DON'T BE SILLY, UNCLE GABBY, EVERYONE KNOWS THAT AN ANT CAN LIFT 100 TIMES HIS OWN WEIGHT!
WHEN THEY CRAWL INSIDE ME THROUGH MY BUSTED HEAD THEY FILL MY ARMS AND LEGS, AND THEIR STRENGTH, COMBINED WITH THE "MAGIC OF DOLLIES" ENABLES THEM TO LIFT AND THROW HUGE OBJECTS!!
BUT WHY, INCHES? WHY ARE THEY DOING THESE TERRIBLE THINGS?!

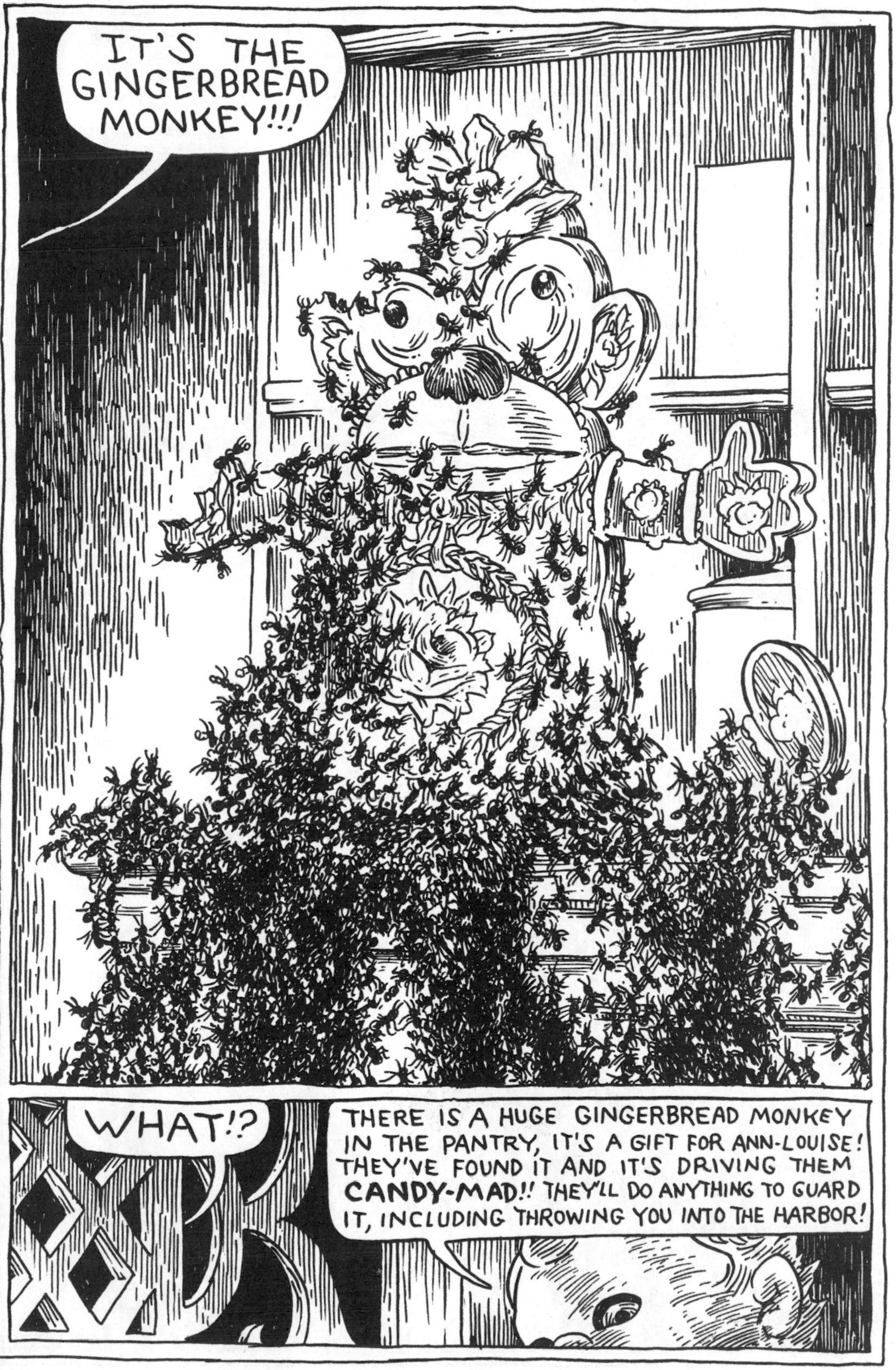
IT'S THE GINGERBREAD MONKEY!!!
WHAT!?
THERE IS A HUGE GINGERBREAD MONKEY IN THE PANTRY, IT'S A GIFT FOR ANN-LOUISE! THEY'VE FOUND IT AND IT'S DRIVING THEM CANDY-MAD!! THEY'LL DO ANYTHING TO GUARD IT, INCLUDING THROWING YOU INTO THE HARBOR!

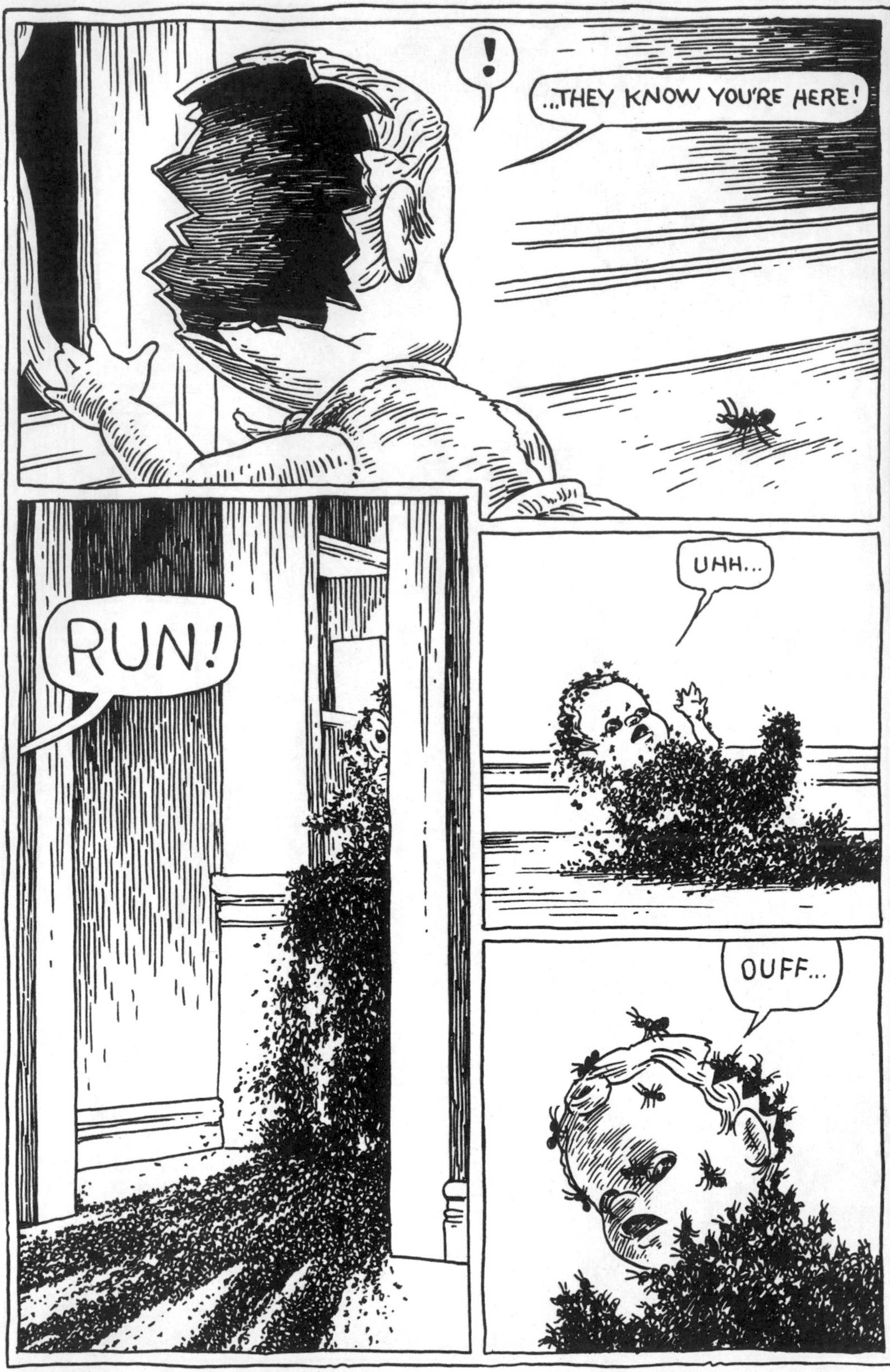
!
...THEY KNOW YOU'RE HERE!
RUN!
UHH...
OUFF...

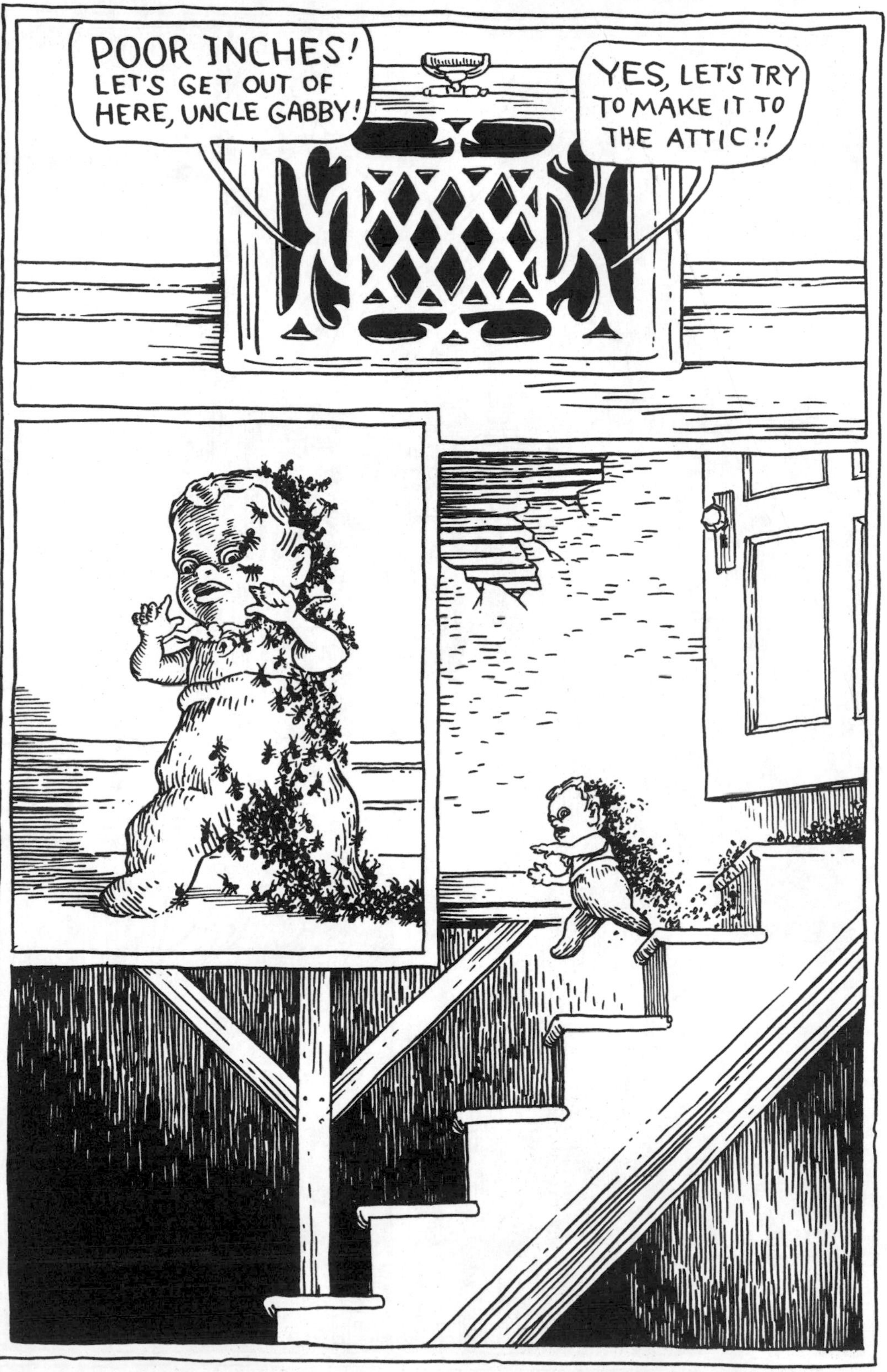
POOR INCHES! LET'S GET OUT OF HERE, UNCLE GABBY!
YES, LET'S TRY TO MAKE IT TO THE ATTIC!!

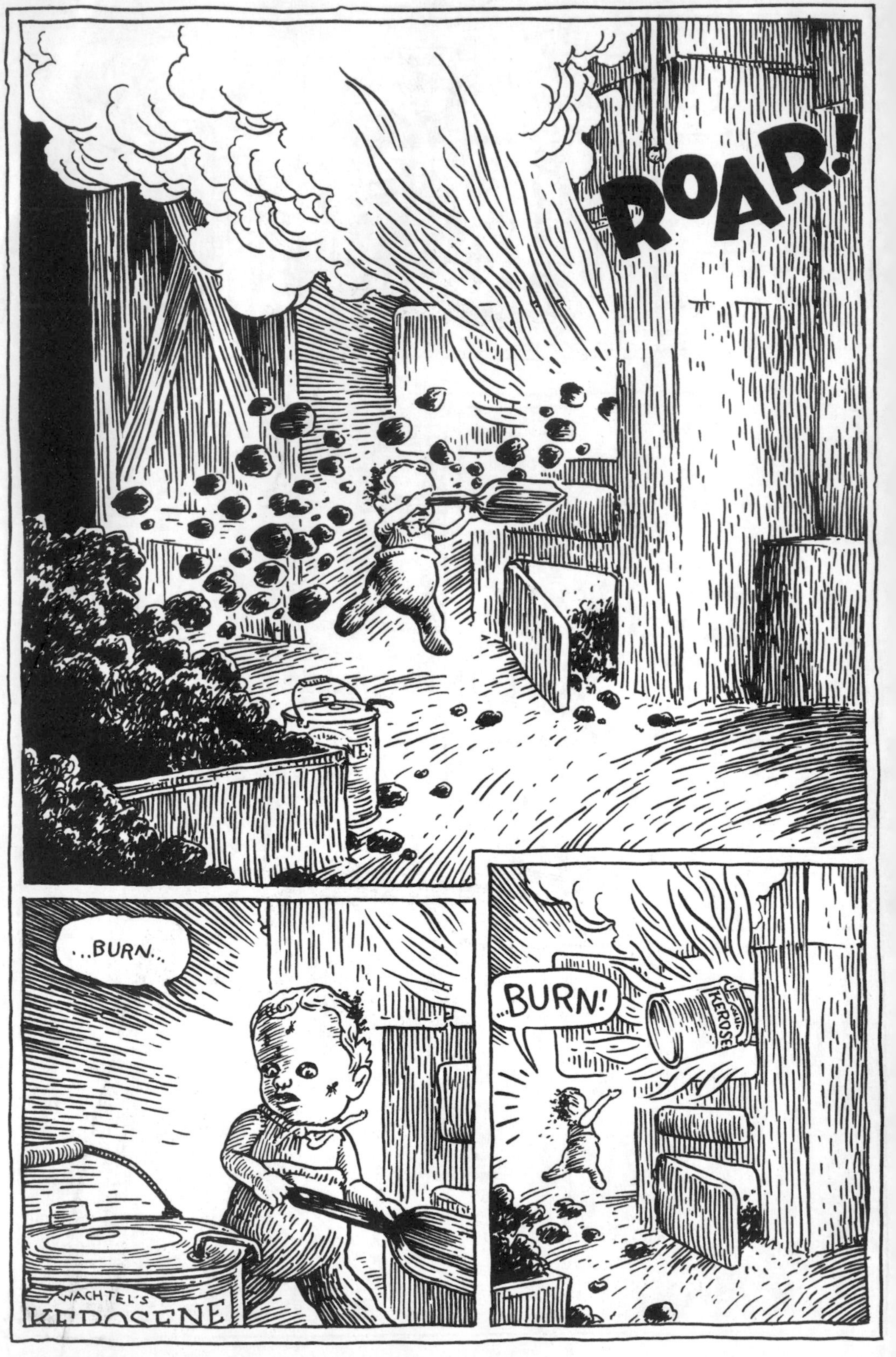
ROAR!
...BURN...
WACHTEL'S
KEROSENE
...BURN!

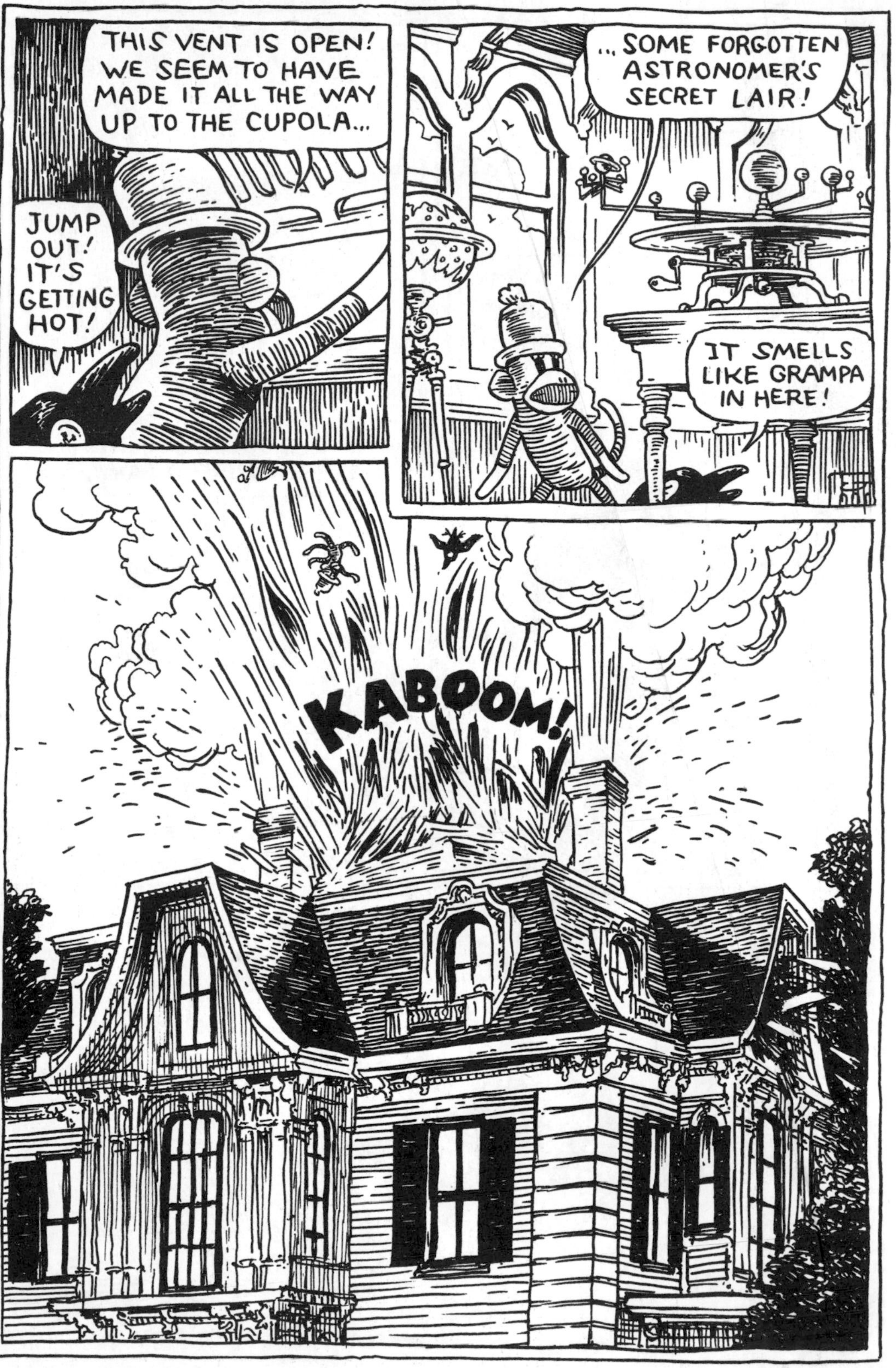
THIS VENT IS OPEN! WE SEEM TO HAVE MADE IT ALL THE WAY UP TO THE CUPOLA...
JUMP OUT! IT'S GETTING HOT!
...SOME FORGOTTEN ASTRONOMER'S SECRET LAIR!
IT SMELLS LIKE GRAMPA IN HERE!
KABOOM!

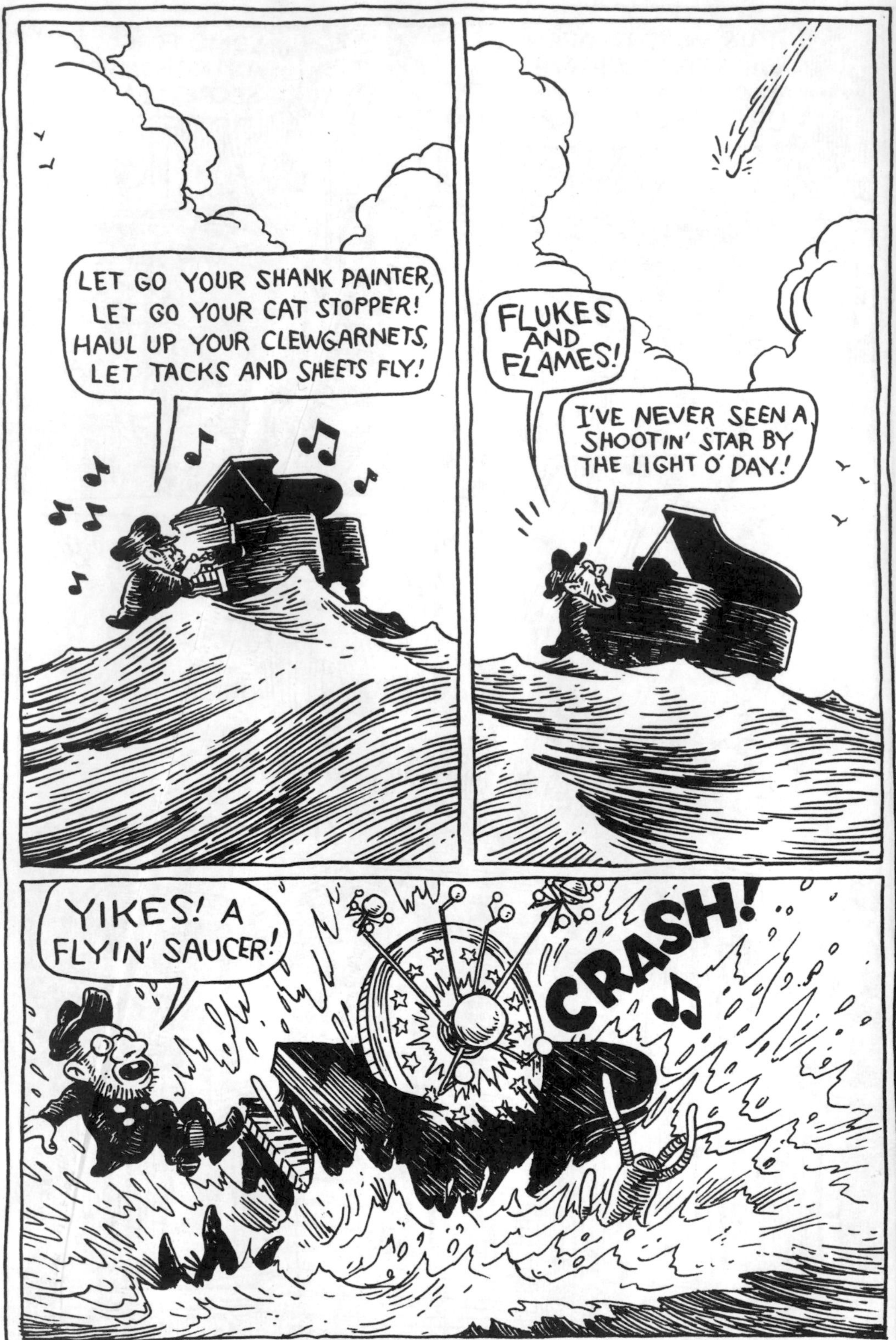
LET GO YOUR SHANK PAINTER, LET GO YOUR CAT STOPPER! HAUL UP YOUR CLEWGARNETS, LET TACKS AND SHEETS FLY!
FLUKES AND FLAMES!
I'VE NEVER SEEN A SHOOTIN' STAR BY THE LIGHT O' DAY!
YIKES! A FLYIN' SAUCER!
CRASH!

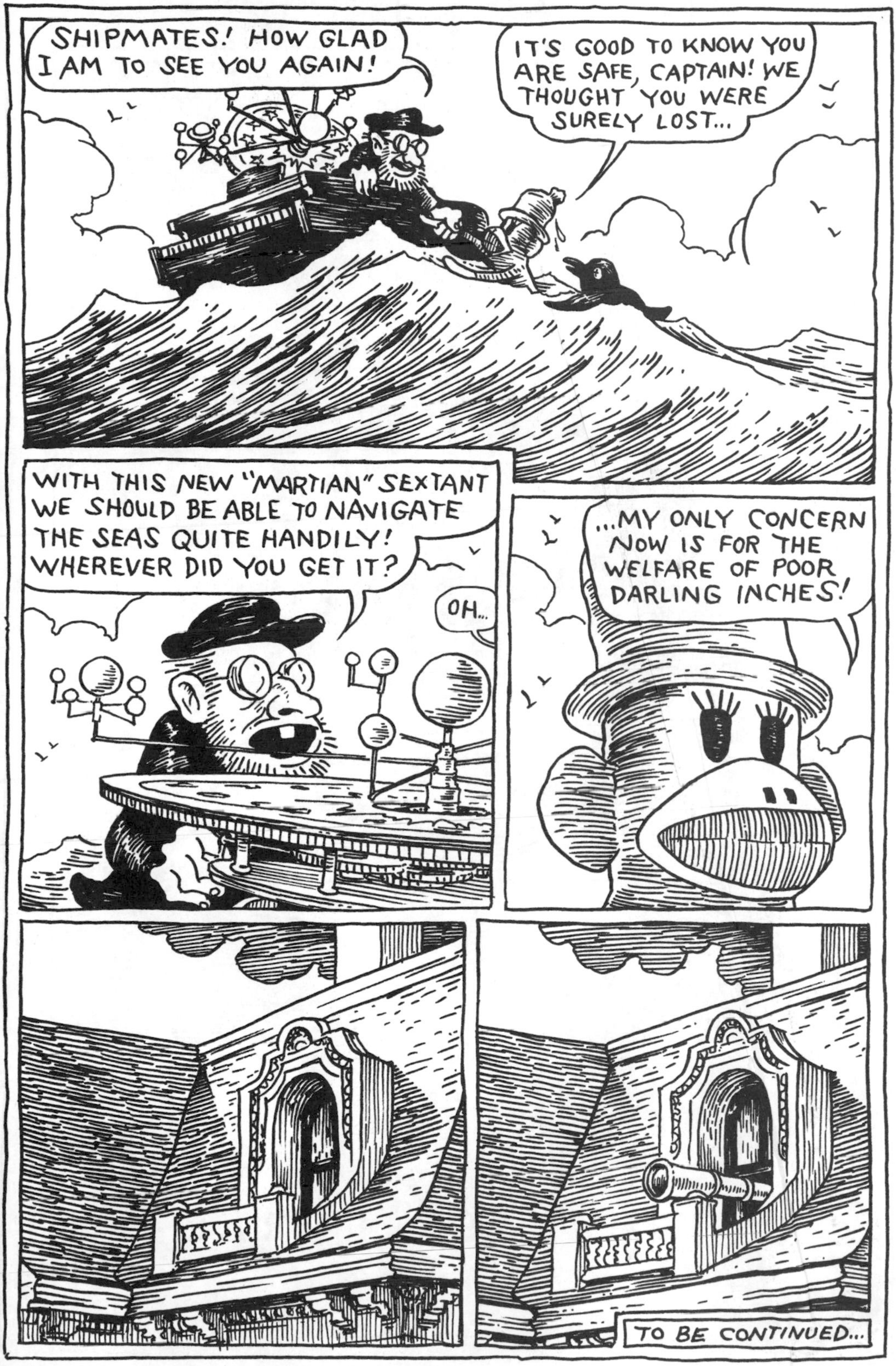
SHIPMATES! HOW GLAD I AM TO SEE YOU AGAIN!
IT'S GOOD TO KNOW YOU ARE SAFE, CAPTAIN! WE THOUGHT YOU WERE SURELY LOST...
WITH THIS NEW "MARTIAN" SEXTANT WE SHOULD BE ABLE TO NAVIGATE THE SEAS QUITE HANDILY! WHEREVER DID YOU GET IT?
OH...
...MY ONLY CONCERN NOW IS FOR THE WELFARE OF POOR DARLING INCHES!
TO BE CONTINUED...

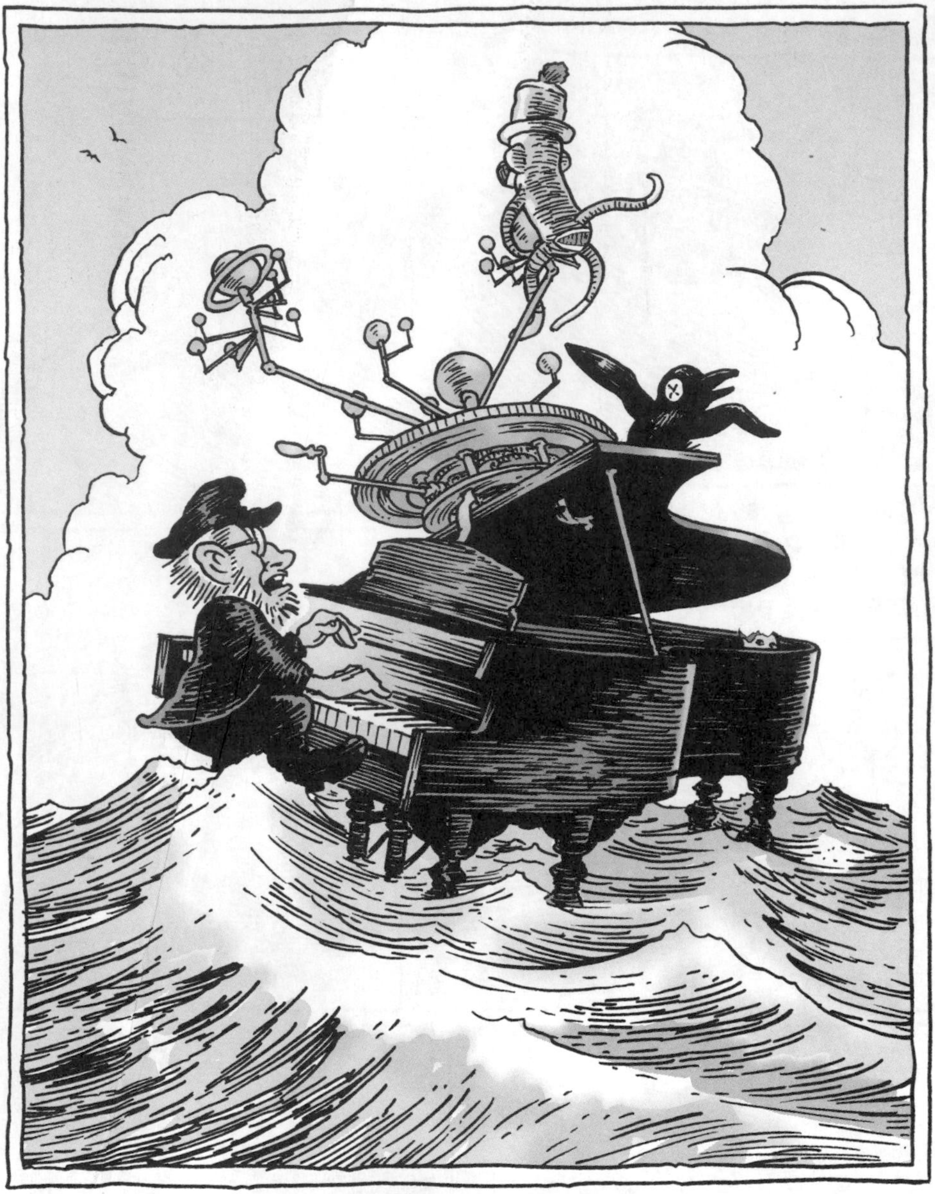

Chapter Three

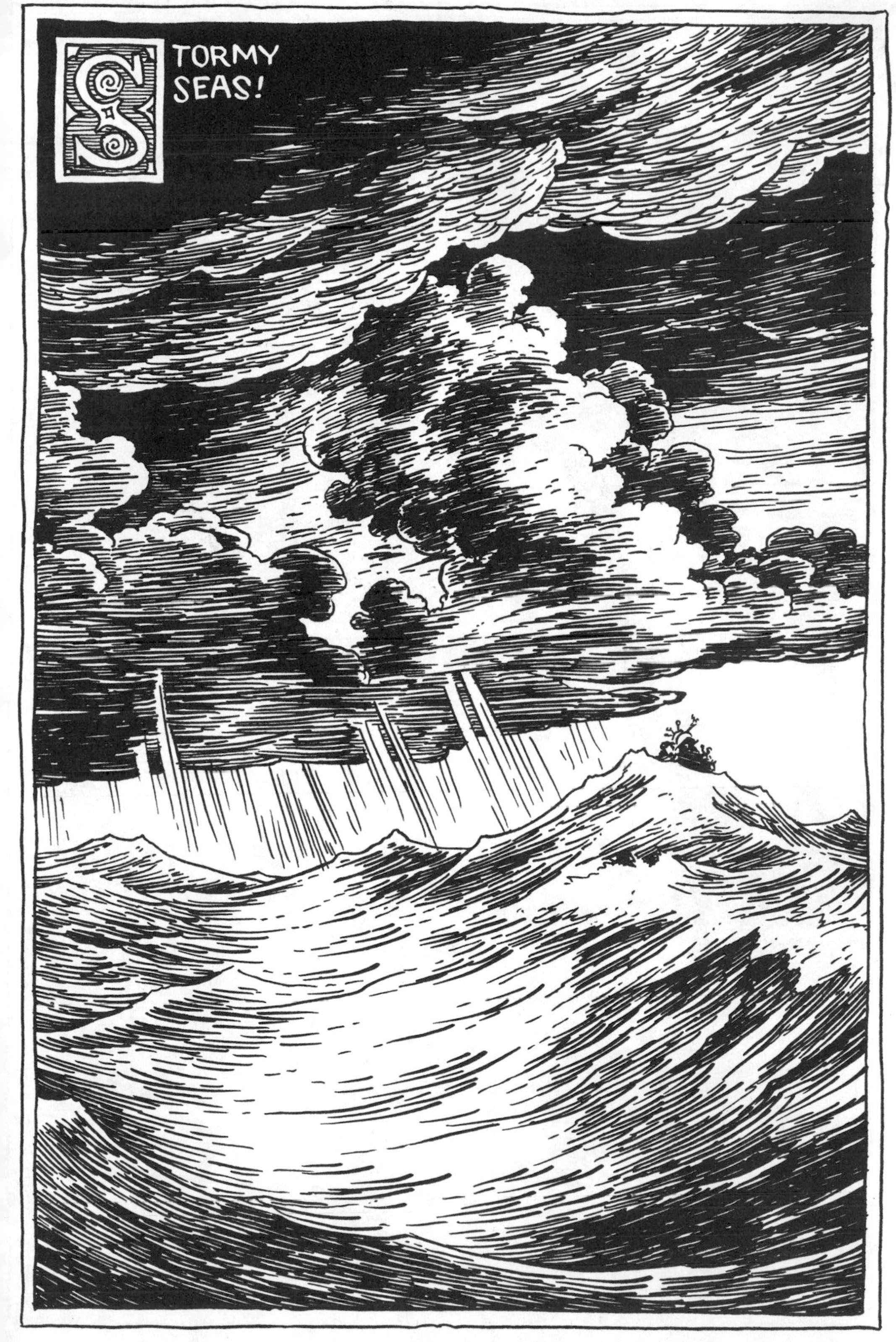
STORMY
SEAS!

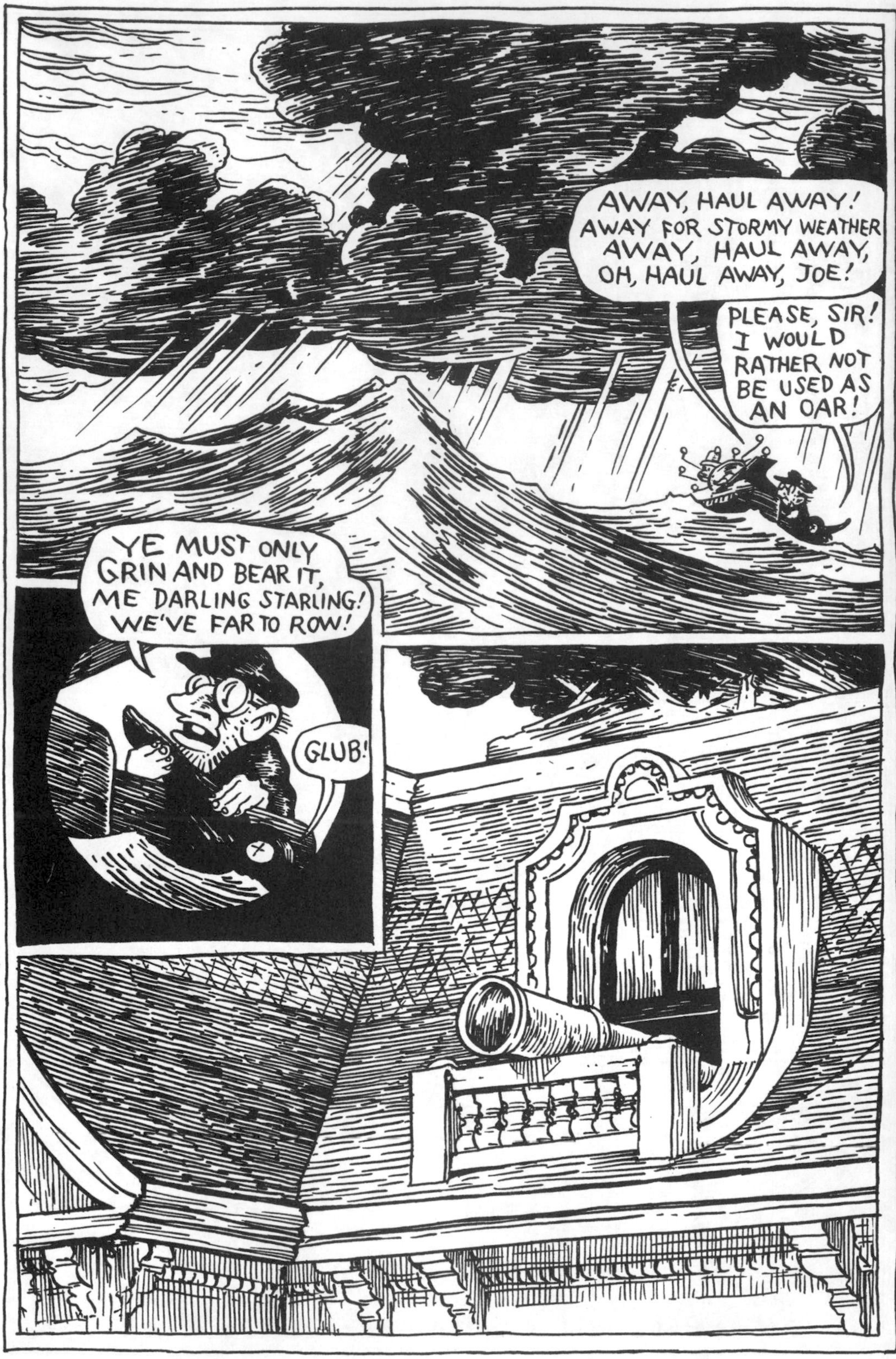
AWAY, HAUL AWAY! AWAY FOR STORMY WEATHER AWAY, HAUL AWAY, OH, HAUL AWAY, JOE!
PLEASE, SIR! I WOULD RATHER NOT BE USED AS AN OAR!
YE MUST ONLY GRIN AND BEAR IT, ME DARLING STARLING! WE'VE FAR TO ROW!
GLUB!

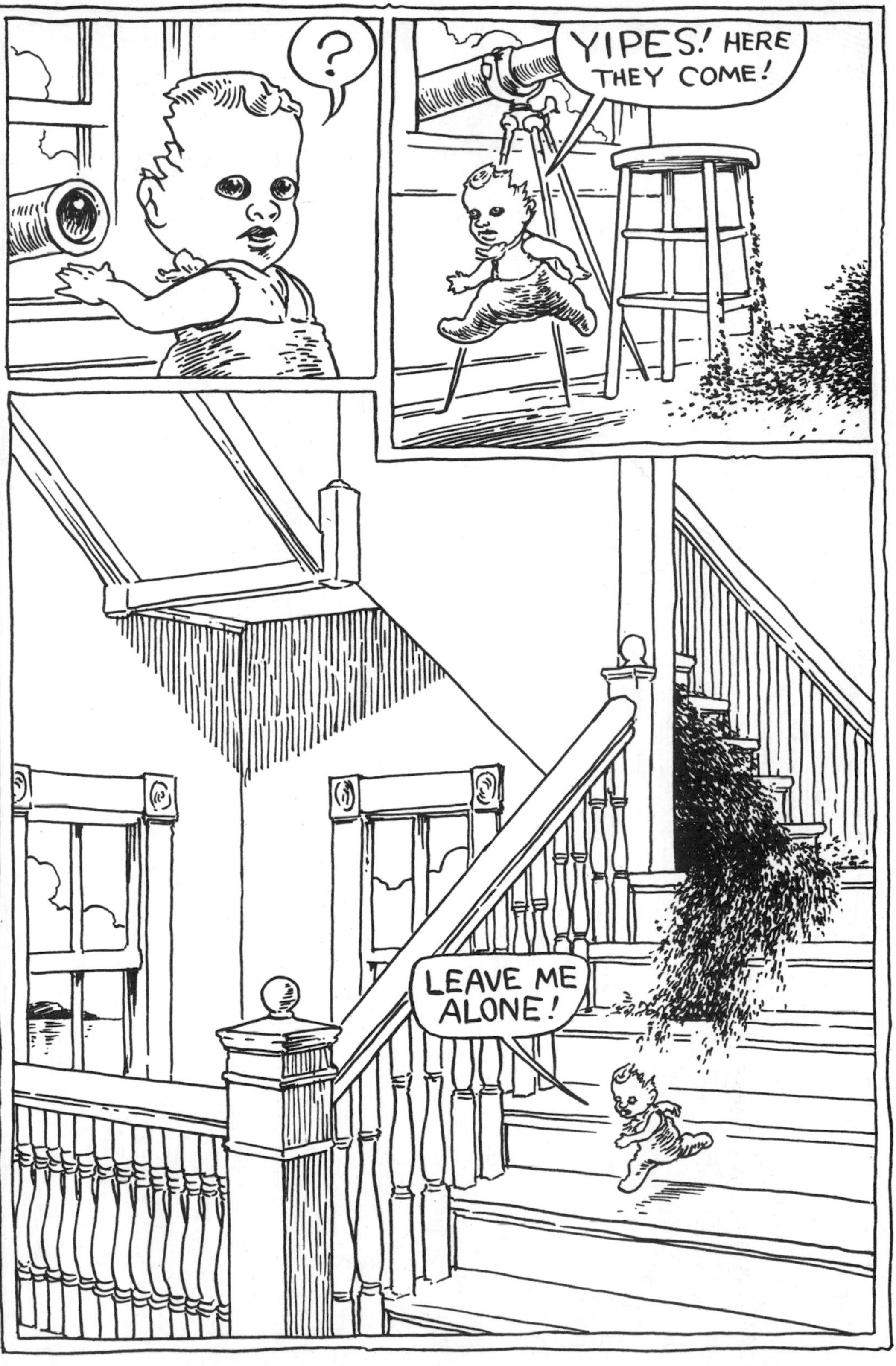
?
YIPES! HERE THEY COME!
LEAVE ME ALONE!

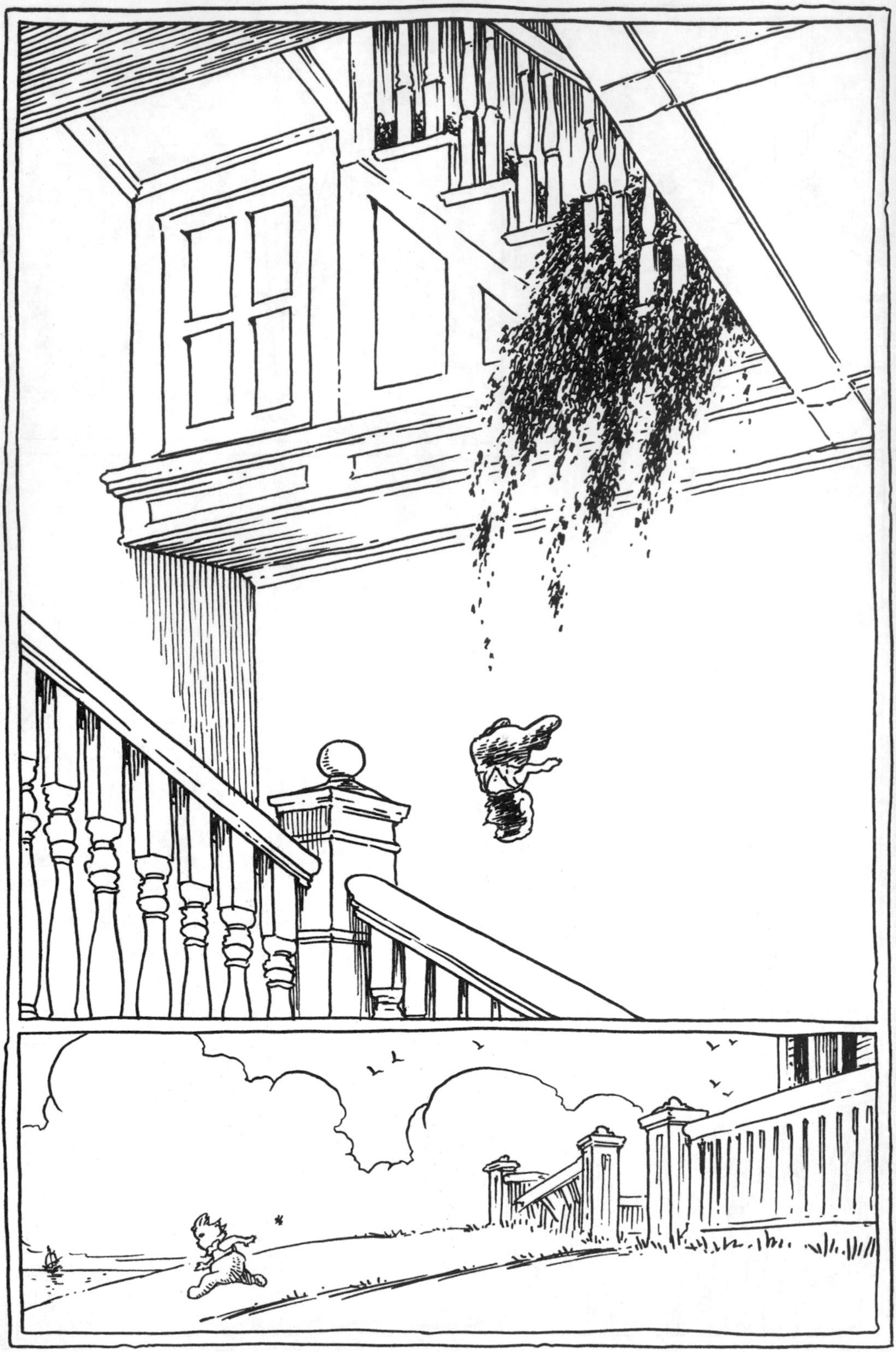

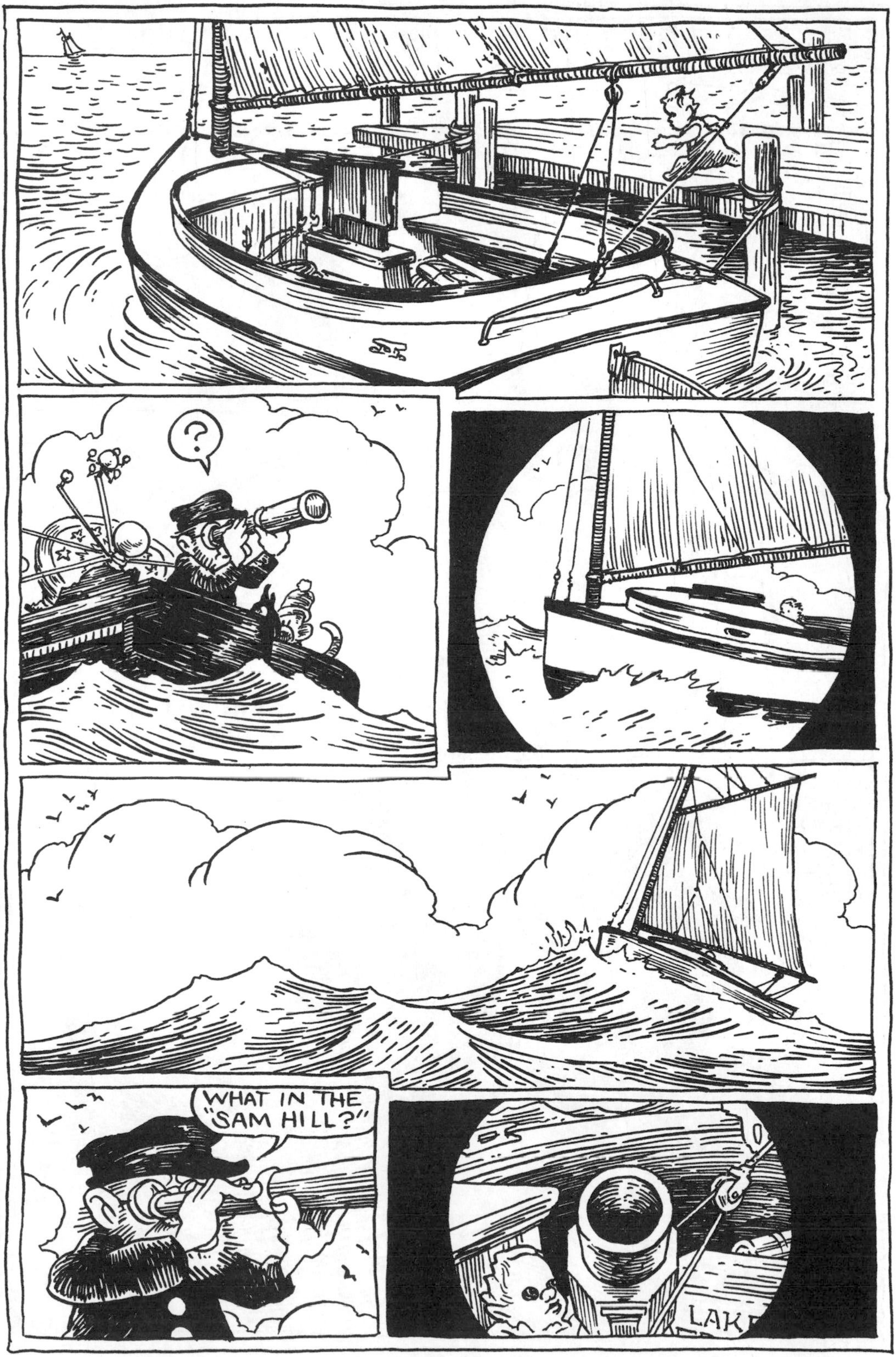
?
WHAT IN THE "SAM HILL?"
LAK

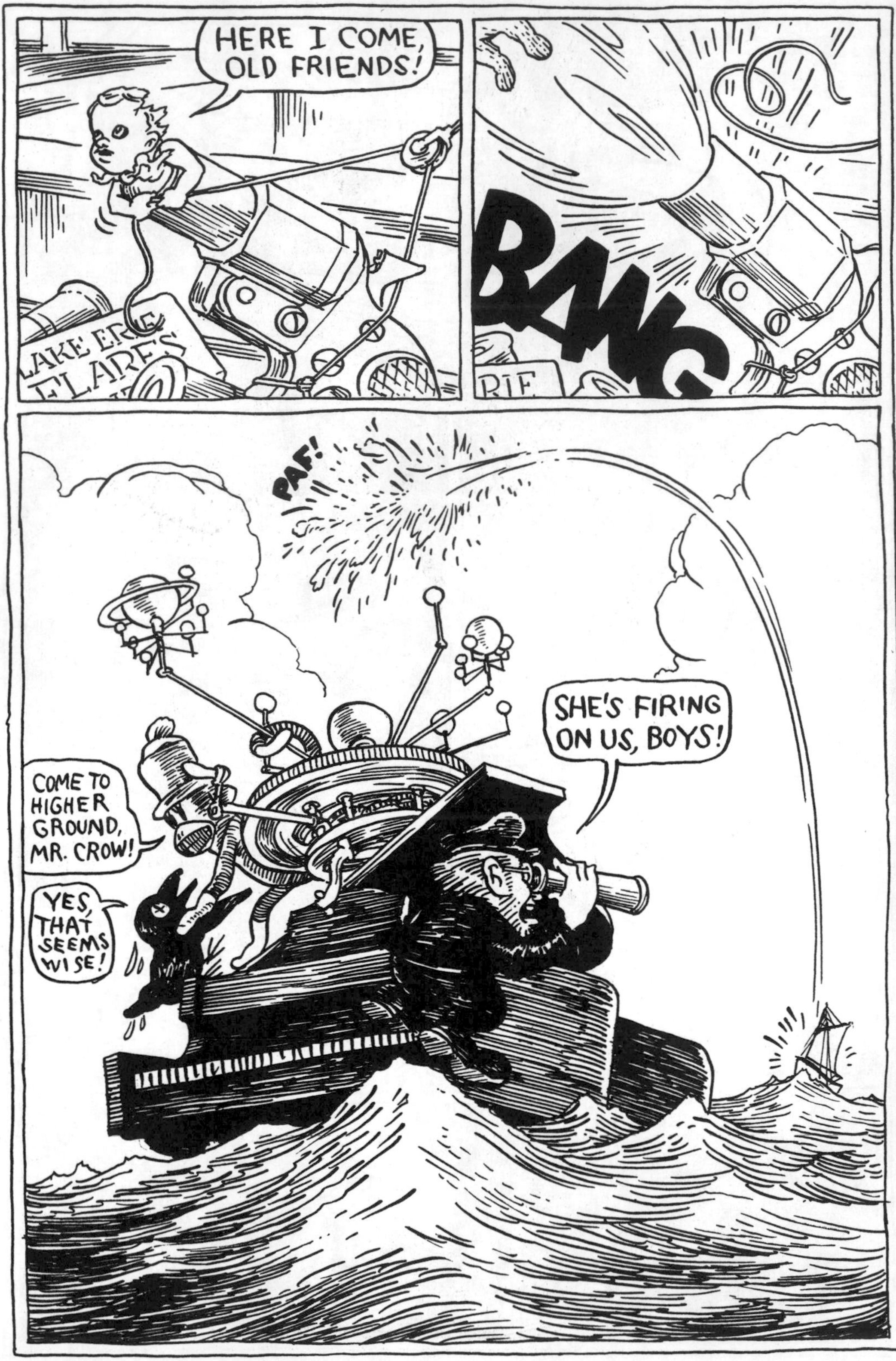
HERE I COME, OLD FRIENDS!
LAKE ERIE FLARES
BANG
ERIE
PAF!
SHE'S FIRING ON US, BOYS!
COME TO HIGHER GROUND, MR. CROW!
YES, THAT SEEMS WISE!

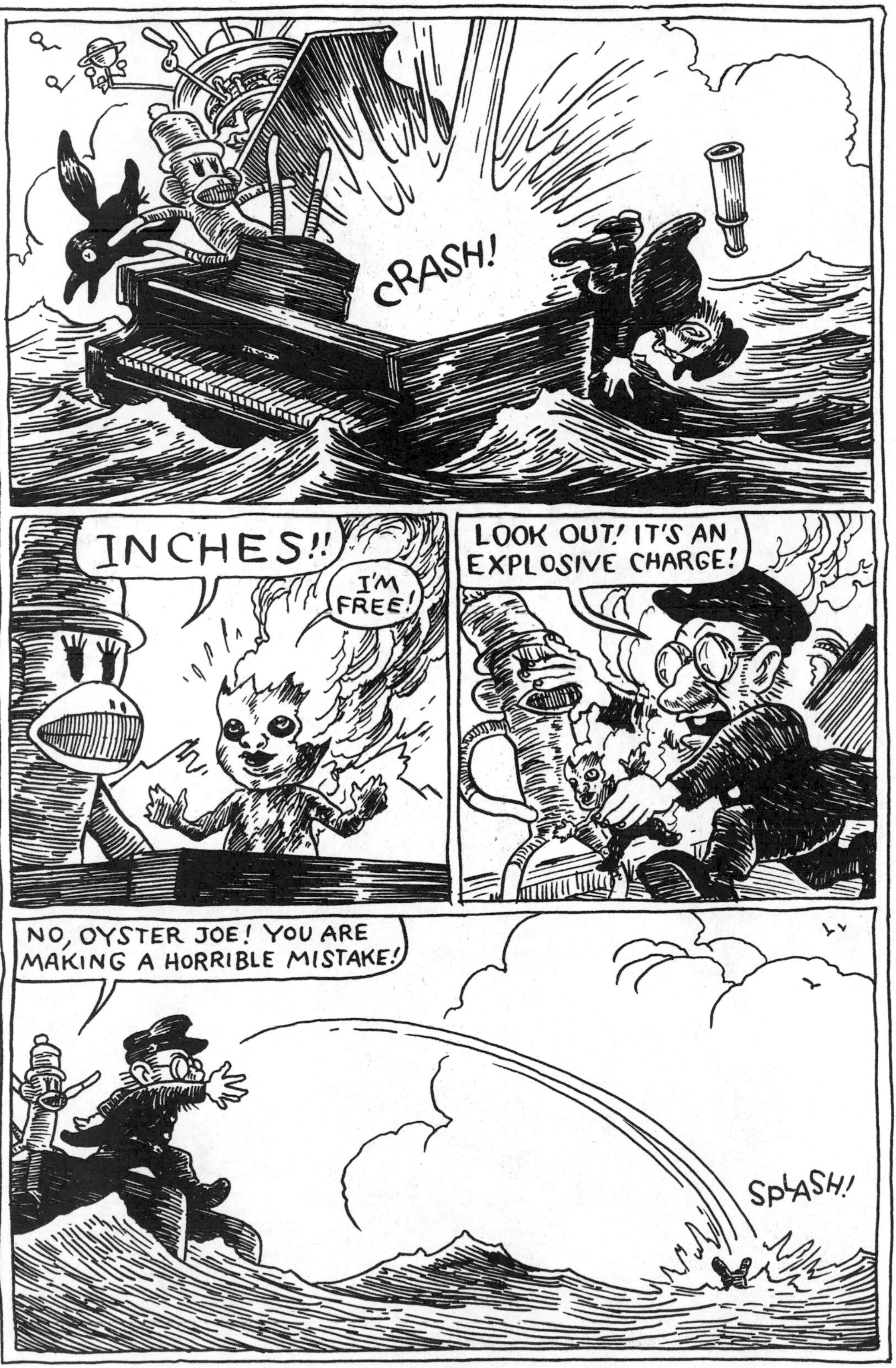
CRASH!
INCHES!!
I'M FREE!
LOOK OUT! IT'S AN EXPLOSIVE CHARGE!
NO, OYSTER JOE! YOU ARE MAKING A HORRIBLE MISTAKE!
SPLASH!

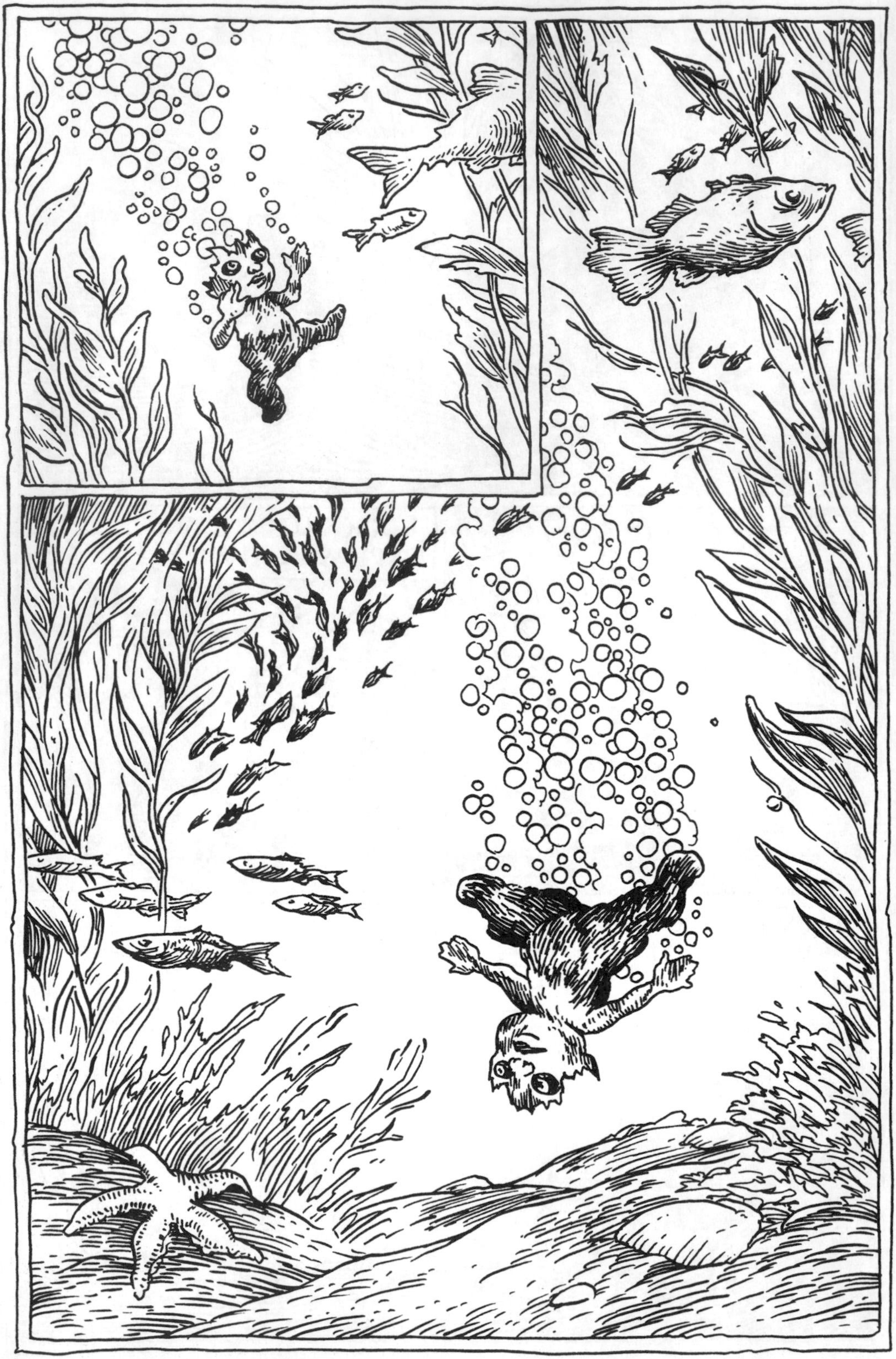

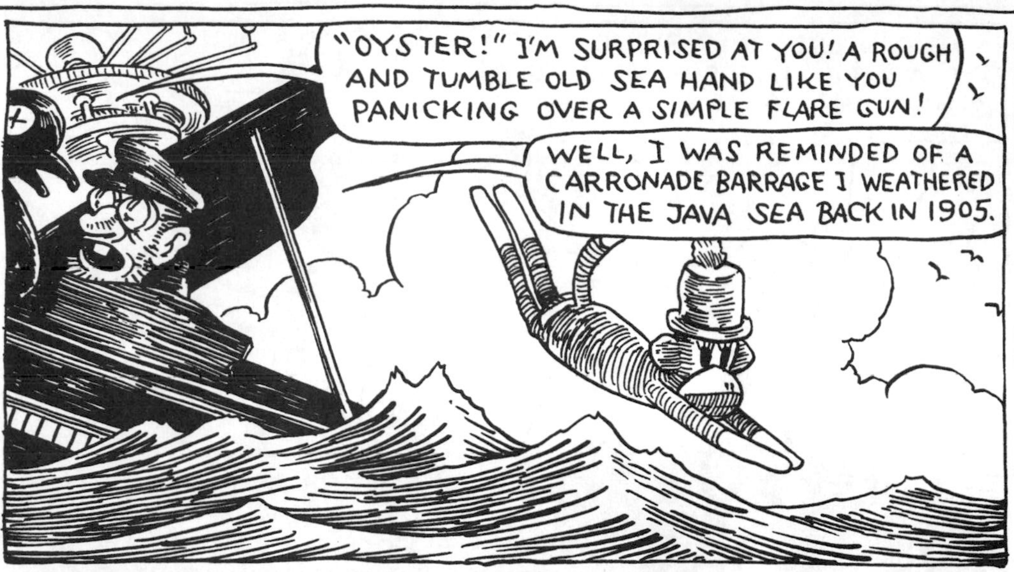
"OYSTER!" I'M SURPRISED AT YOU! A ROUGH AND TUMBLE OLD SEA HAND LIKE YOU PANICKING OVER A SIMPLE FLARE GUN!
WELL, I WAS REMINDED OF A CARRONADE BARRAGE I WEATHERED IN THE JAVA SEA BACK IN 1905.

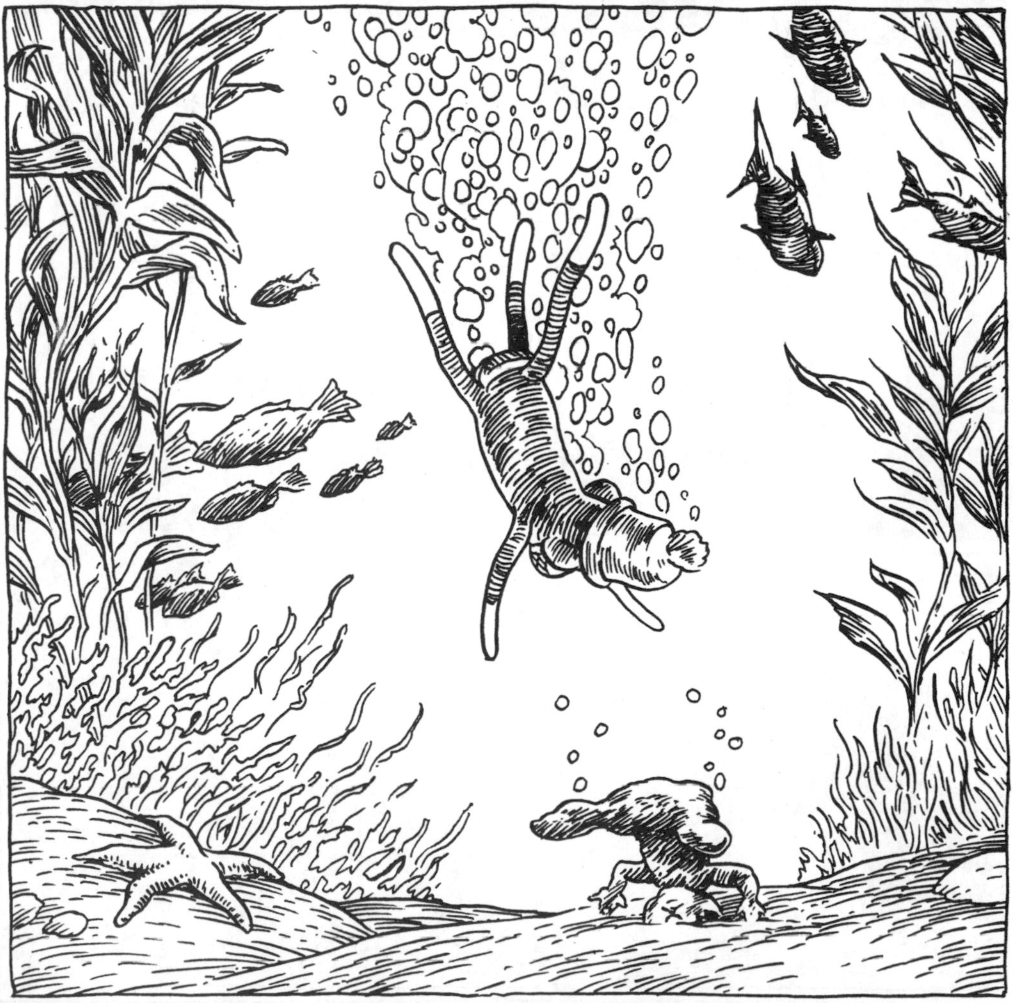

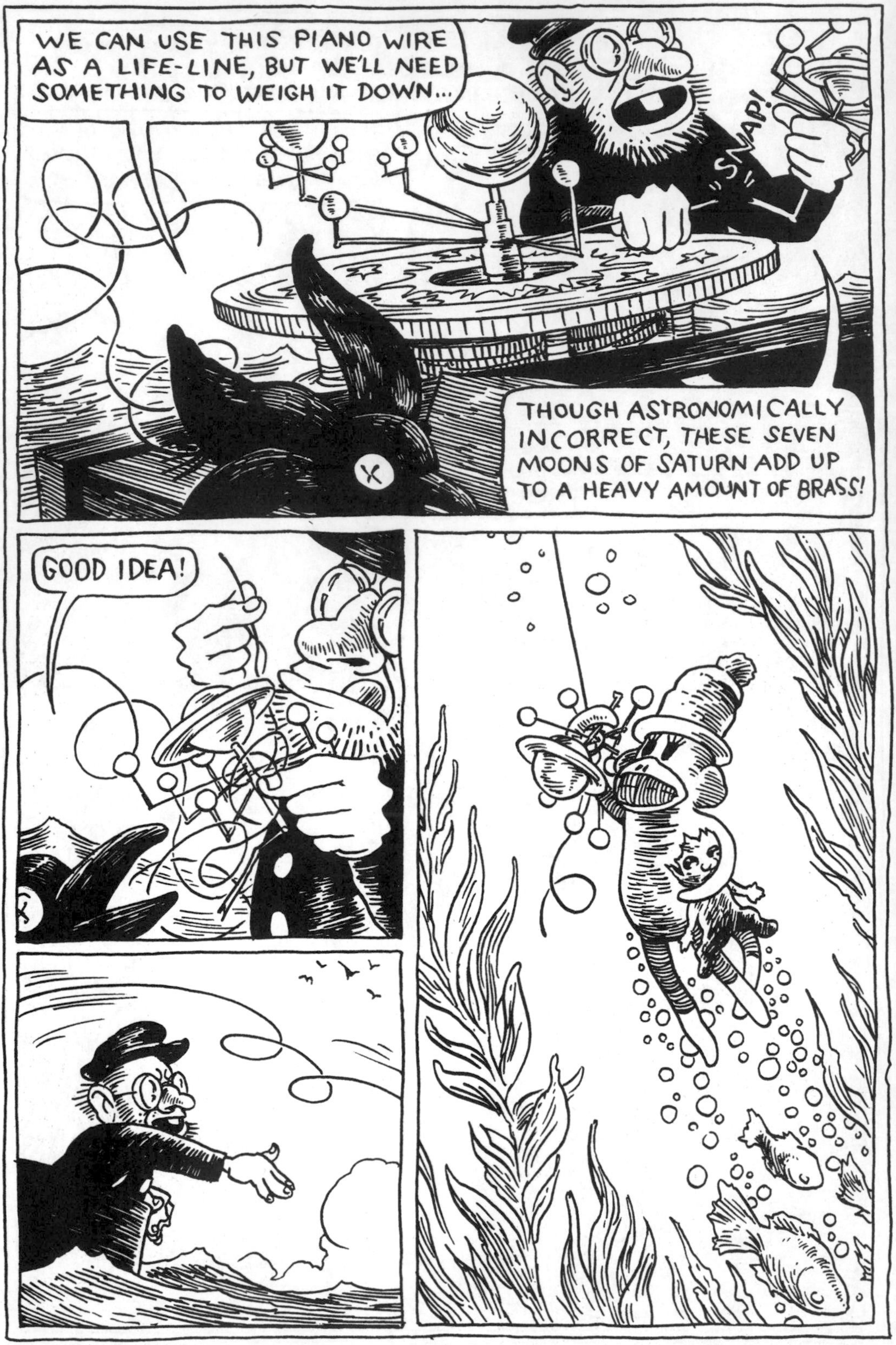
WE CAN USE THIS PIANO WIRE AS A LIFE-LINE, BUT WE'LL NEED SOMETHING TO WEIGH IT DOWN...
SNAP!
THOUGH ASTRONOMICALLY INCORRECT, THESE SEVEN MOONS OF SATURN ADD UP TO A HEAVY AMOUNT OF BRASS!
GOOD IDEA!

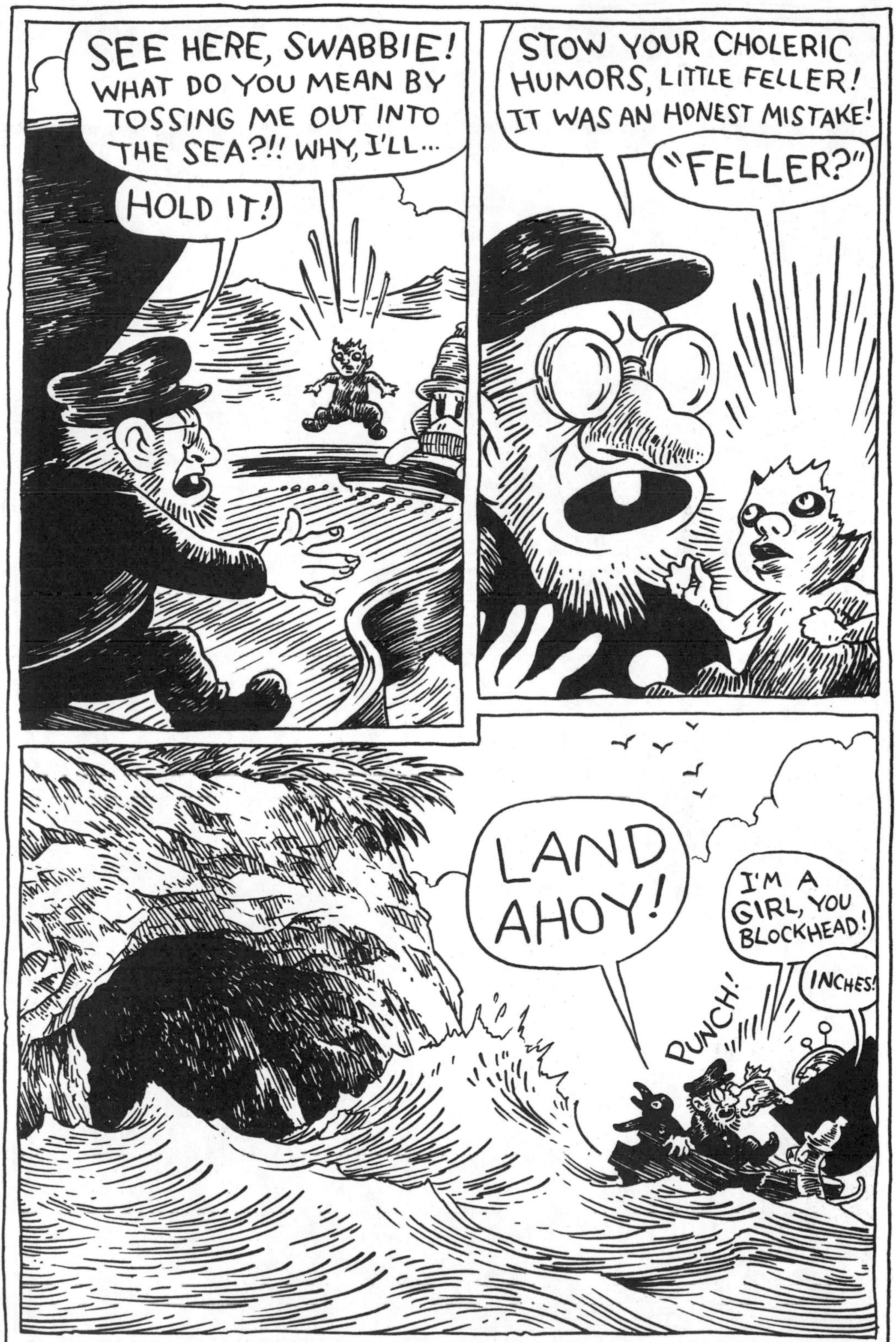
SEE HERE, SWABBIE! WHAT DO YOU MEAN BY TOSSING ME OUT INTO THE SEA?!! WHY, I'LL...
HOLD IT!
STOW YOUR CHOLERIC HUMORS, LITTLE FELLER! IT WAS AN HONEST MISTAKE!
"FELLER?"
LAND AHOY!
I'M A GIRL, YOU BLOCKHEAD!
PUNCH!
INCHES!

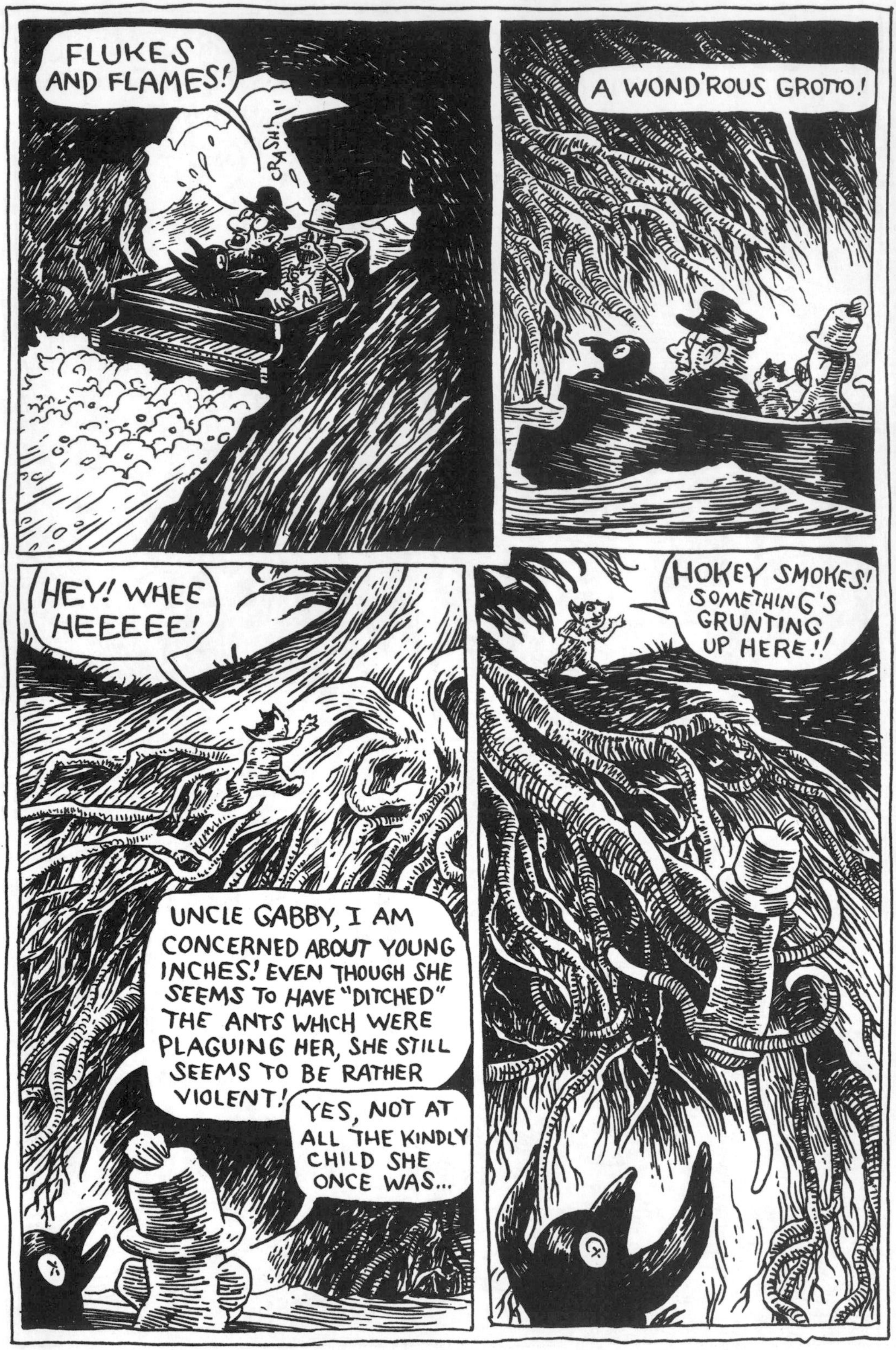
FLUKES AND FLAMES!
CRASH!
A WOND'ROUS GROTTO!
HEY! WHEE HEEEEEE!
UNCLE GABBY, I AM CONCERNED ABOUT YOUNG INCHES! EVEN THOUGH SHE SEEMS TO HAVE "DITCHED" THE ANTS WHICH WERE PLAGUING HER, SHE STILL SEEMS TO BE RATHER VIOLENT!
YES, NOT AT ALL THE KINDLY CHILD SHE ONCE WAS...
HOKEY SMOKES! SOMETHING'S GRUNTING UP HERE!!

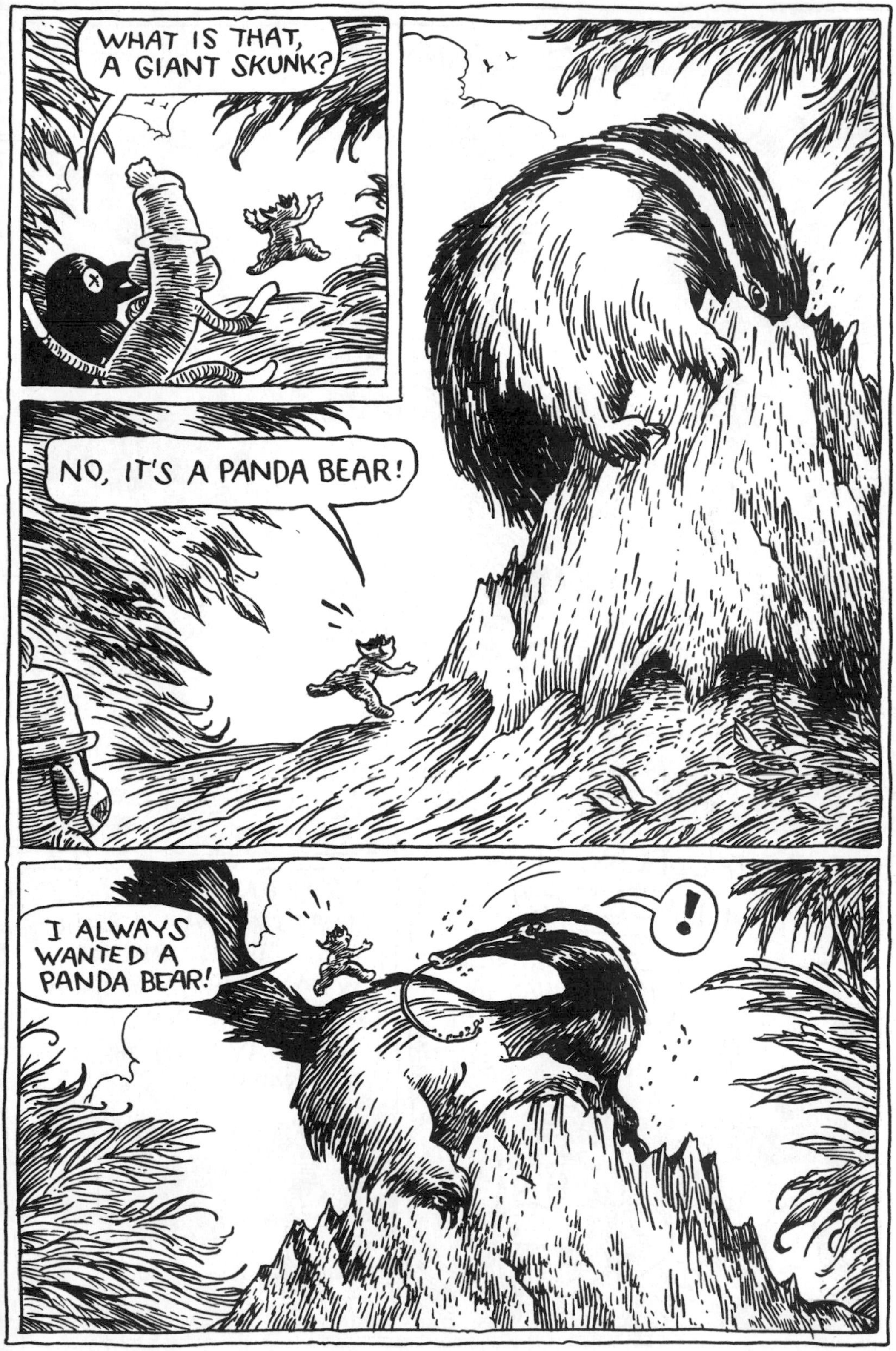
WHAT IS THAT, A GIANT SKUNK?
NO, IT'S A PANDA BEAR!
I ALWAYS WANTED A PANDA BEAR!
!

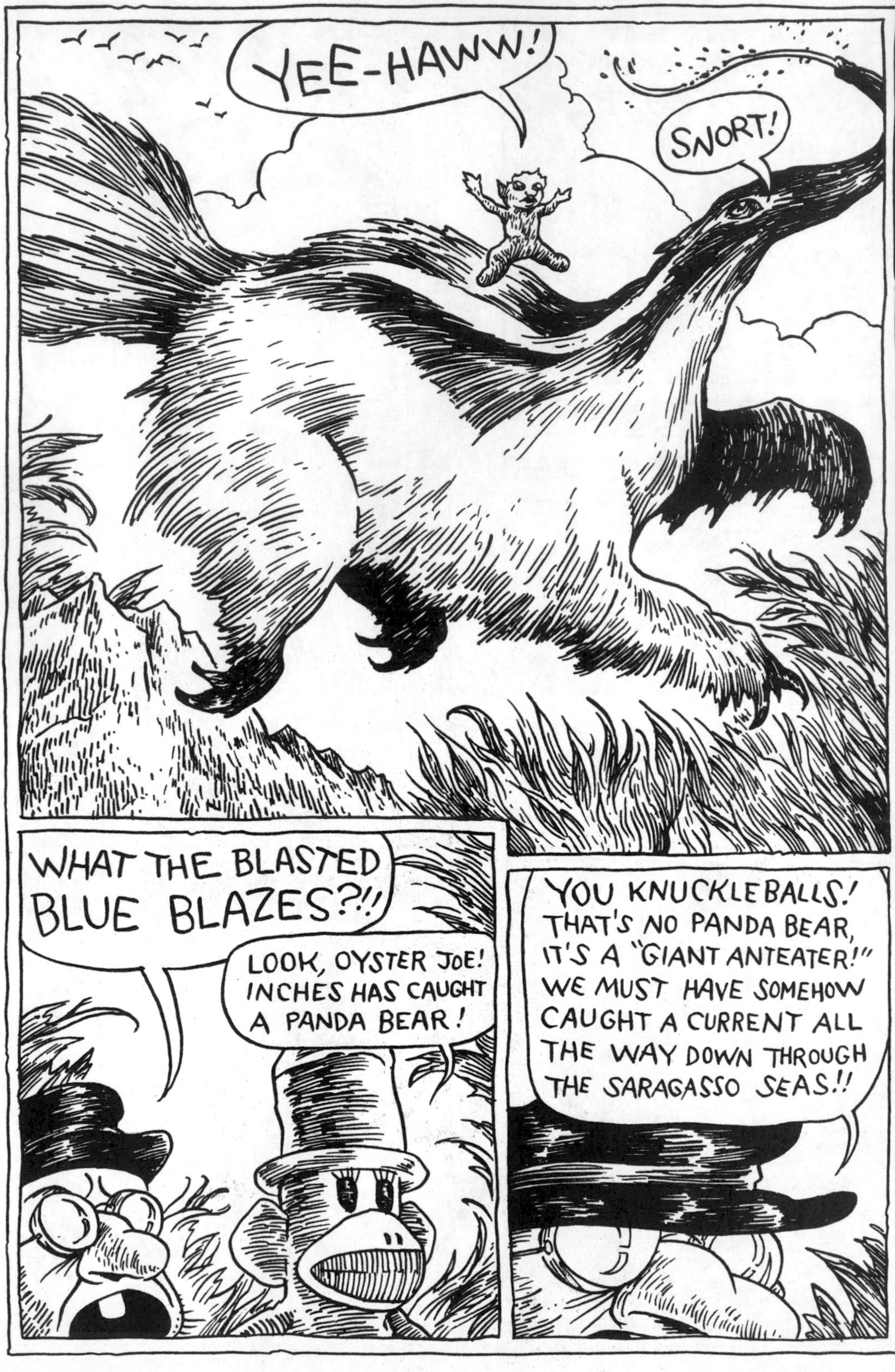
YEE-HAWW!
SNORT!
WHAT THE BLASTED BLUE BLAZES?!!
LOOK, OYSTER JOE! INCHES HAS CAUGHT A PANDA BEAR!
YOU KNUCKLEBALLS! THAT'S NO PANDA BEAR, IT'S A "GIANT ANTEATER!" WE MUST HAVE SOMEHOW CAUGHT A CURRENT ALL THE WAY DOWN THROUGH THE SARAGASSO SEAS!!

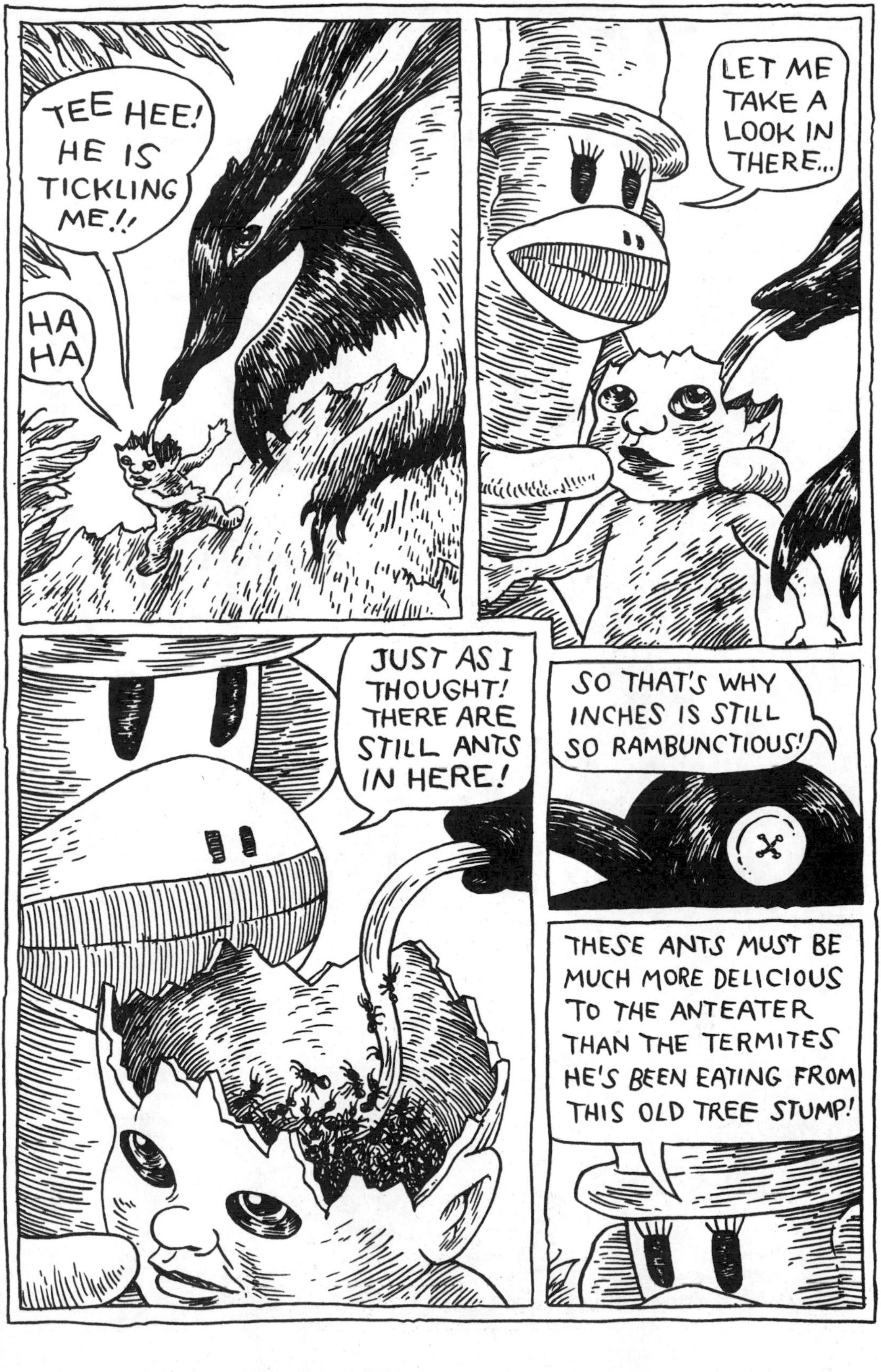
TEE HEE! HE IS TICKLING ME!!
HA HA
LET ME TAKE A LOOK IN THERE...
JUST AS I THOUGHT! THERE ARE STILL ANTS IN HERE!
SO THAT'S WHY INCHES IS STILL SO RAMBUNCTIOUS!
THESE ANTS MUST BE MUCH MORE DELICIOUS TO THE ANTEATER THAN THE TERMITES HE'S BEEN EATING FROM THIS OLD TREE STUMP!

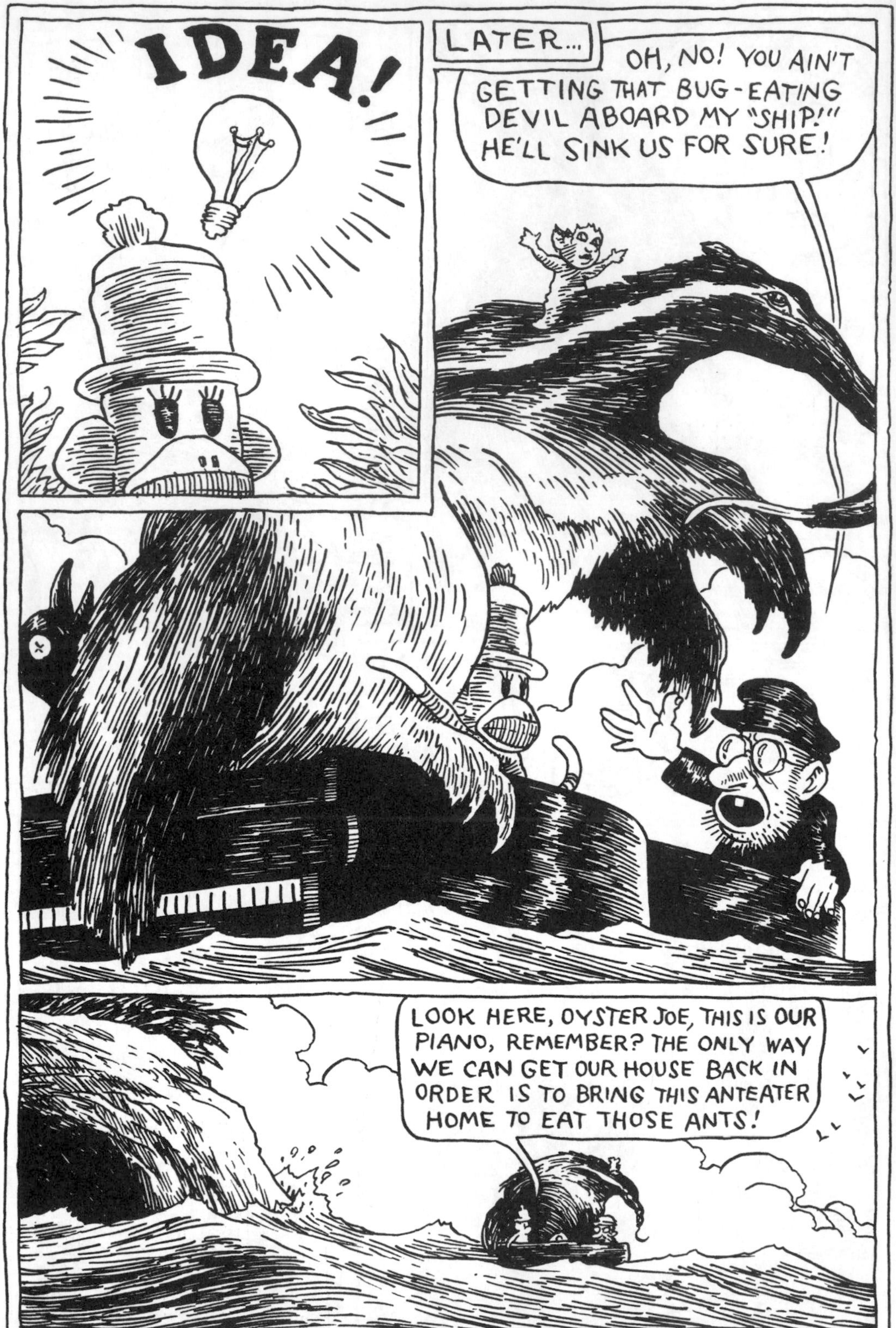
IDEA!
LATER...
OH, NO! YOU AIN'T GETTING THAT BUG-EATING DEVIL ABOARD MY "SHIP!" HE'LL SINK US FOR SURE!
LOOK HERE, OYSTER JOE, THIS IS OUR PIANO, REMEMBER? THE ONLY WAY WE CAN GET OUR HOUSE BACK IN ORDER IS TO BRING THIS ANTEATER HOME TO EAT THOSE ANTS!

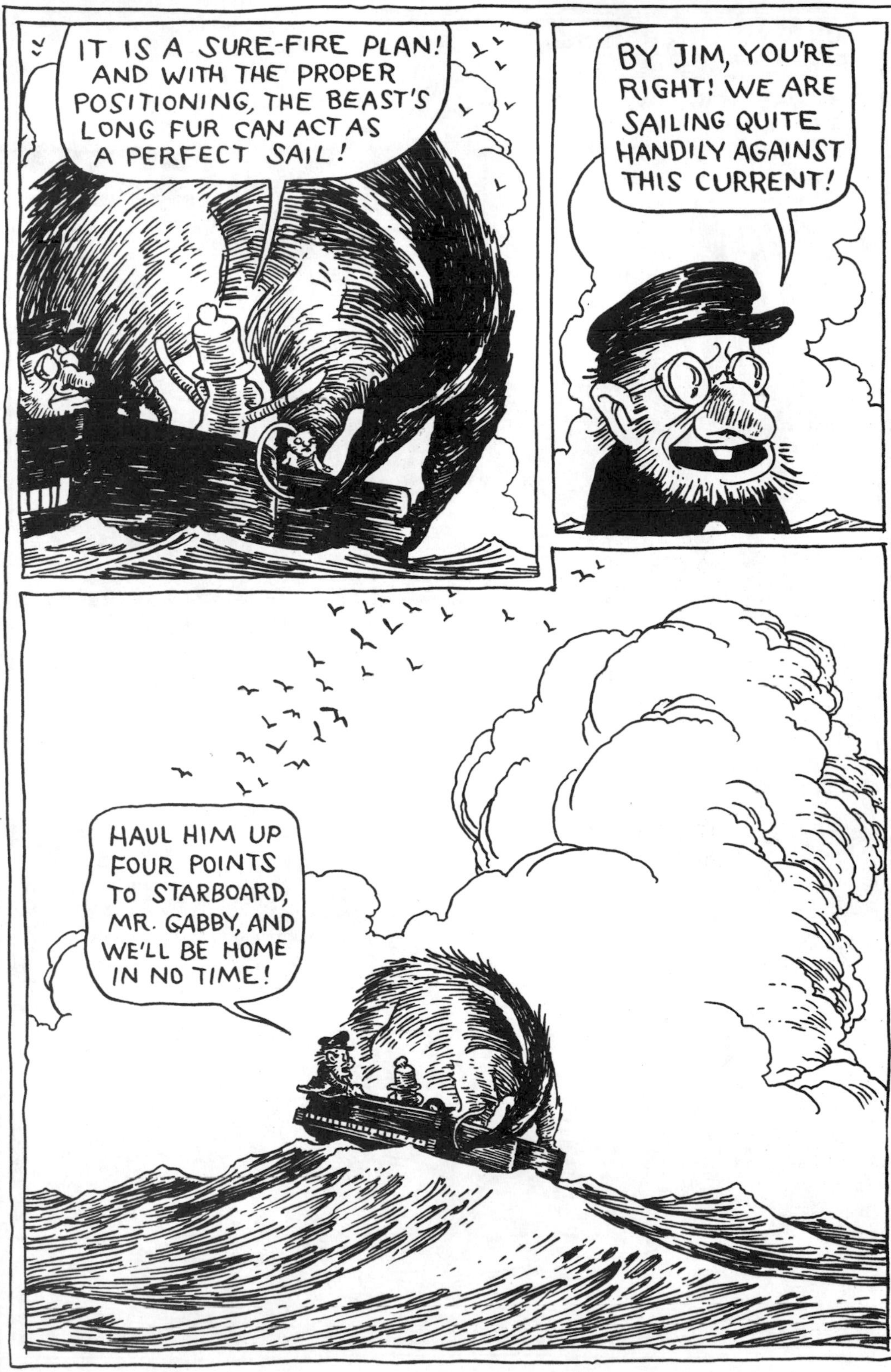
IT IS A SURE-FIRE PLAN! AND WITH THE PROPER POSITIONING, THE BEAST'S LONG FUR CAN ACT AS A PERFECT SAIL!
BY JIM, YOU'RE RIGHT! WE ARE SAILING QUITE HANDILY AGAINST THIS CURRENT!
HAUL HIM UP FOUR POINTS TO STARBOARD, MR. GABBY, AND WE'LL BE HOME IN NO TIME!

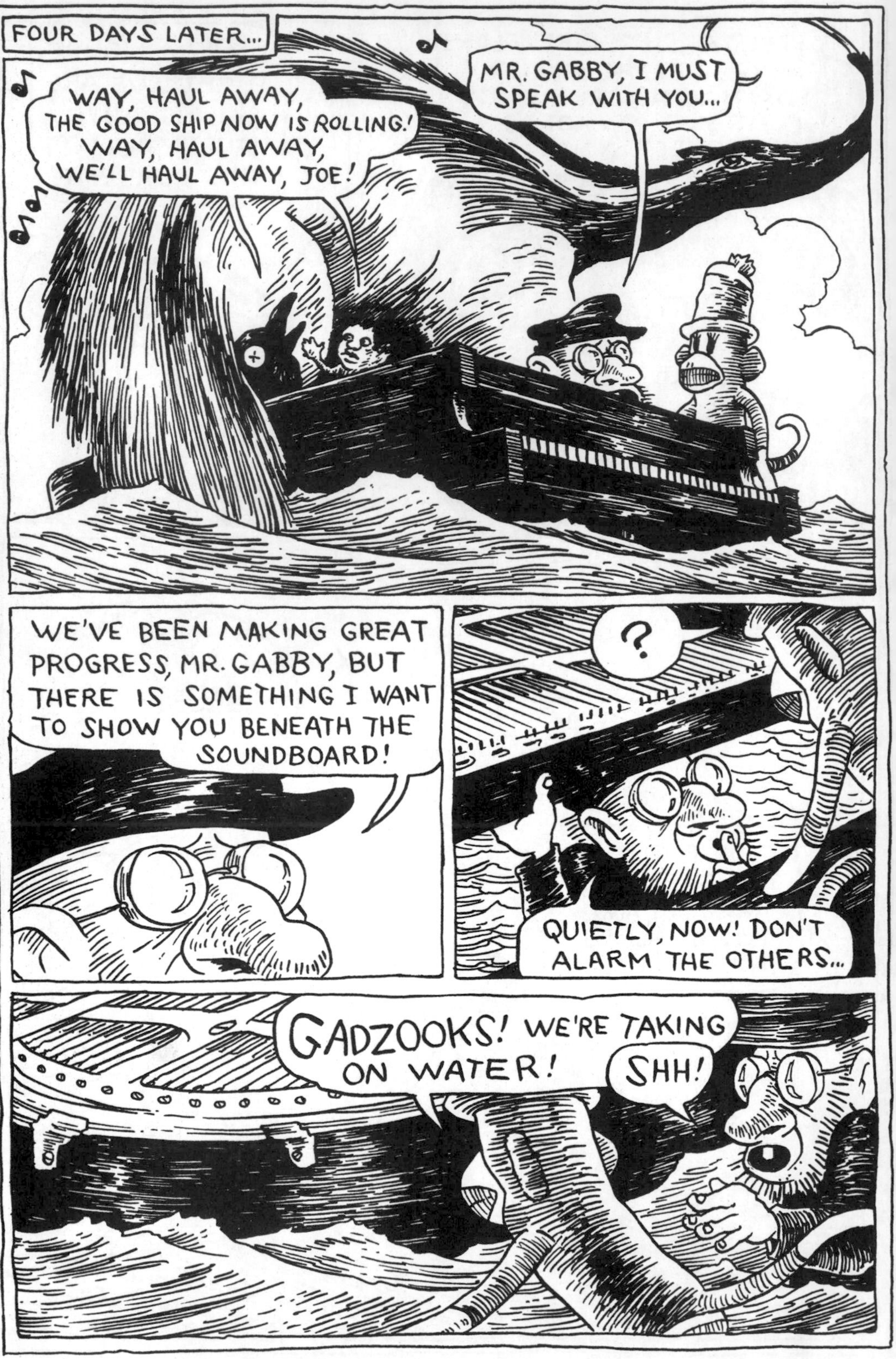
FOUR DAYS LATER...
WAY, HAUL AWAY, THE GOOD SHIP NOW IS ROLLING! WAY, HAUL AWAY, WE'LL HAUL AWAY, JOE!
MR. GABBY, I MUST SPEAK WITH YOU...
WE'VE BEEN MAKING GREAT PROGRESS, MR. GABBY, BUT THERE IS SOMETHING I WANT TO SHOW YOU BENEATH THE SOUNDBOARD!
?
QUIETLY, NOW! DON'T ALARM THE OTHERS...
GADZOOKS! WE'RE TAKING ON WATER!
SHH!

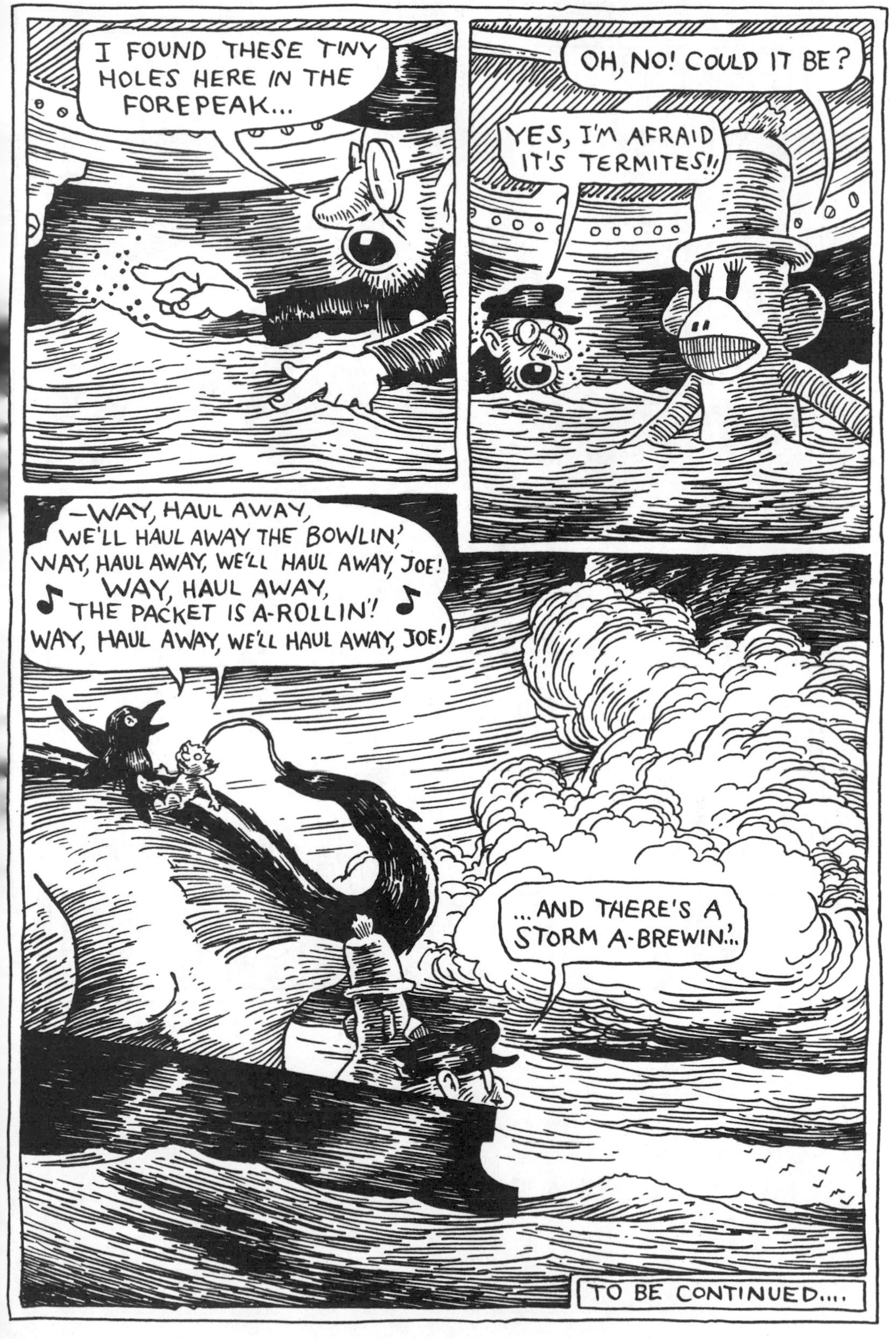
I FOUND THESE TINY HOLES HERE IN THE FOREPEAK...
OH, NO! COULD IT BE?
YES, I'M AFRAID IT'S TERMITES!!
—WAY, HAUL AWAY, WE'LL HAUL AWAY THE BOWLIN', WAY, HAUL AWAY, WE'LL HAUL AWAY, JOE! WAY, HAUL AWAY, THE PACKET IS A-ROLLIN'! WAY, HAUL AWAY, WE'LL HAUL AWAY, JOE!
...AND THERE'S A STORM A-BREWIN'...
TO BE CONTINUED....

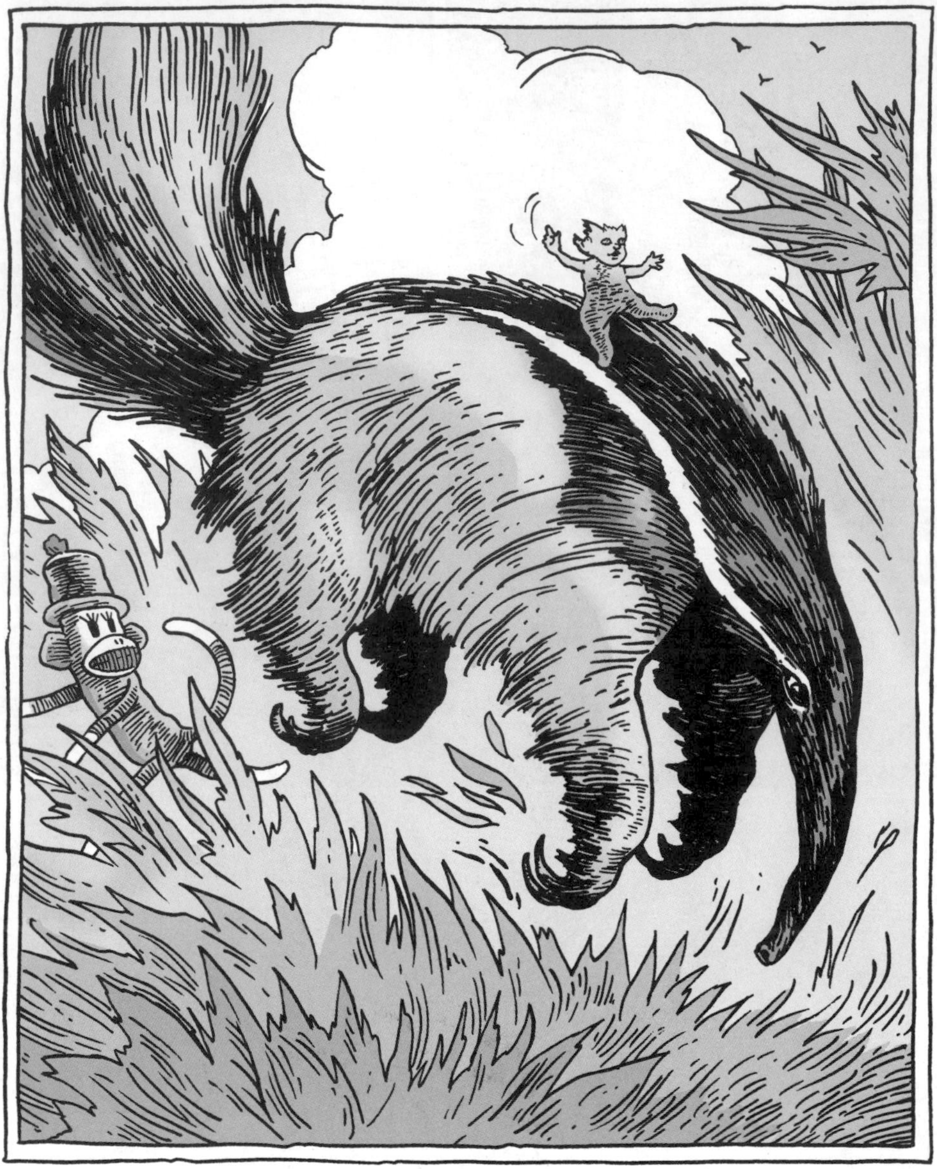

Chapter Four

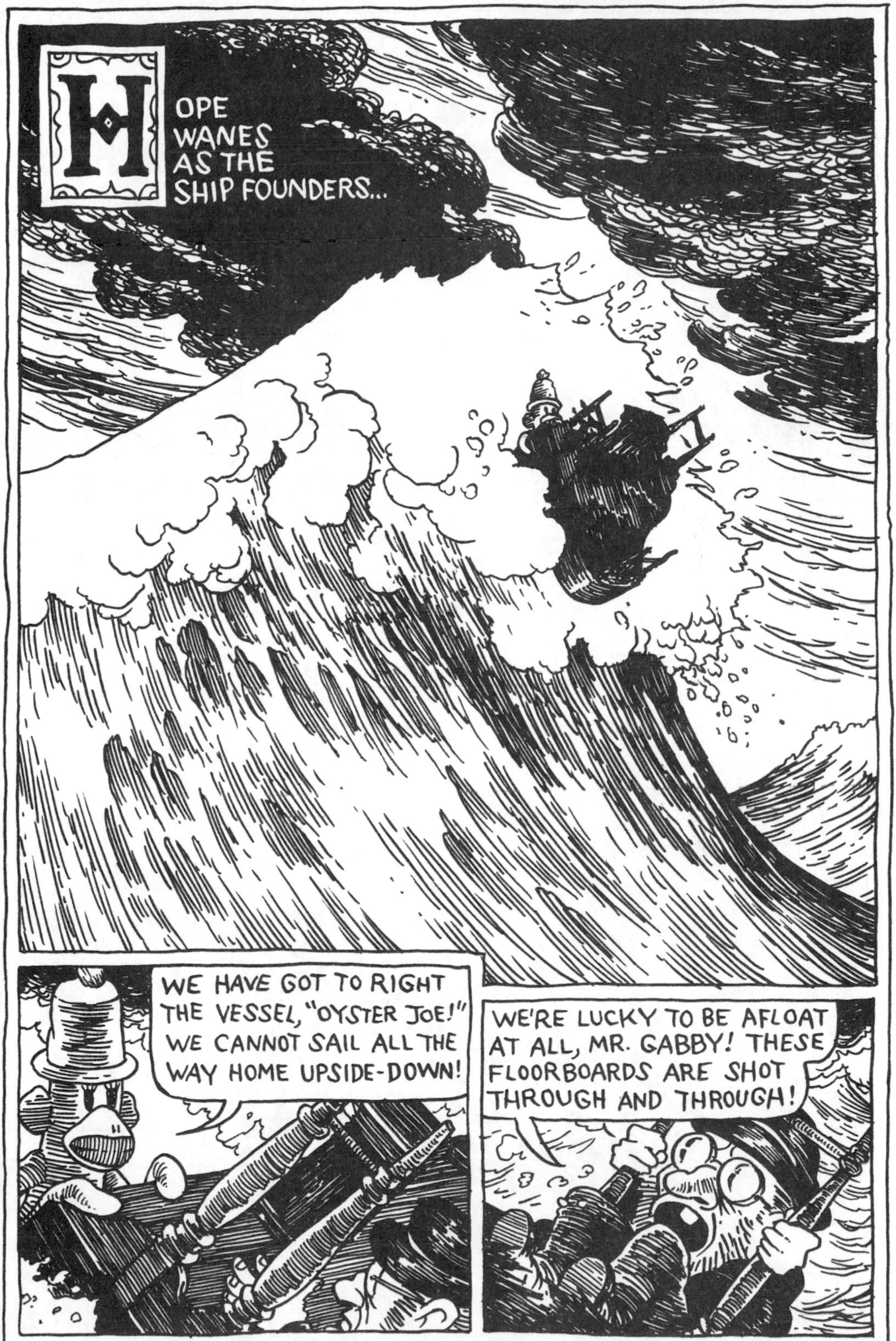
HOPE WANES AS THE SHIP FOUNDERS...
WE HAVE GOT TO RIGHT THE VESSEL, "OYSTER JOE!" WE CANNOT SAIL ALL THE WAY HOME UPSIDE-DOWN!
WE'RE LUCKY TO BE AFLOAT AT ALL, MR. GABBY! THESE FLOORBOARDS ARE SHOT THROUGH AND THROUGH!

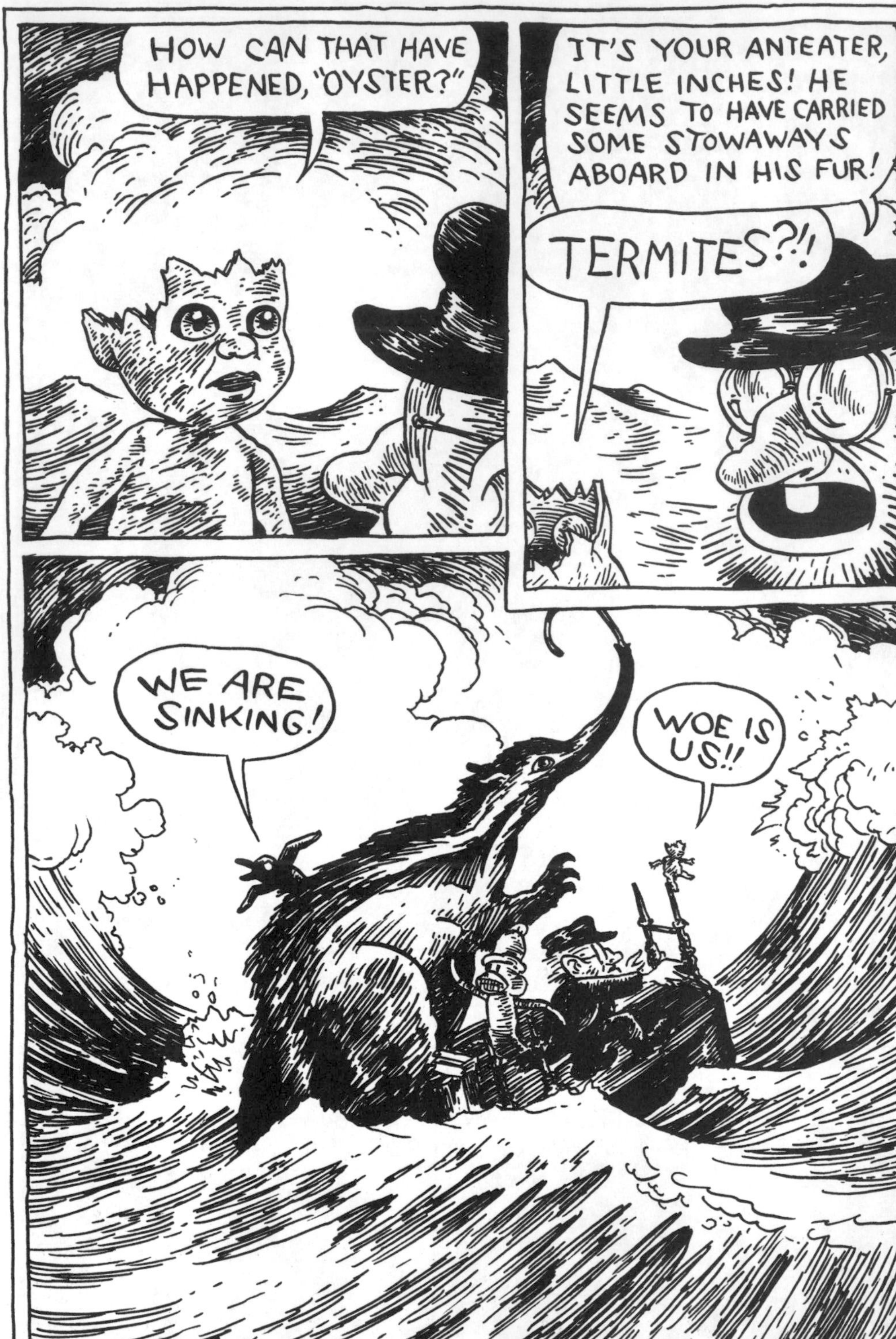
HOW CAN THAT HAVE HAPPENED, "OYSTER?"
IT'S YOUR ANTEATER, LITTLE INCHES! HE SEEMS TO HAVE CARRIED SOME STOWAWAYS ABOARD IN HIS FUR!
TERMITES?!
WE ARE SINKING!
WOE IS US!!

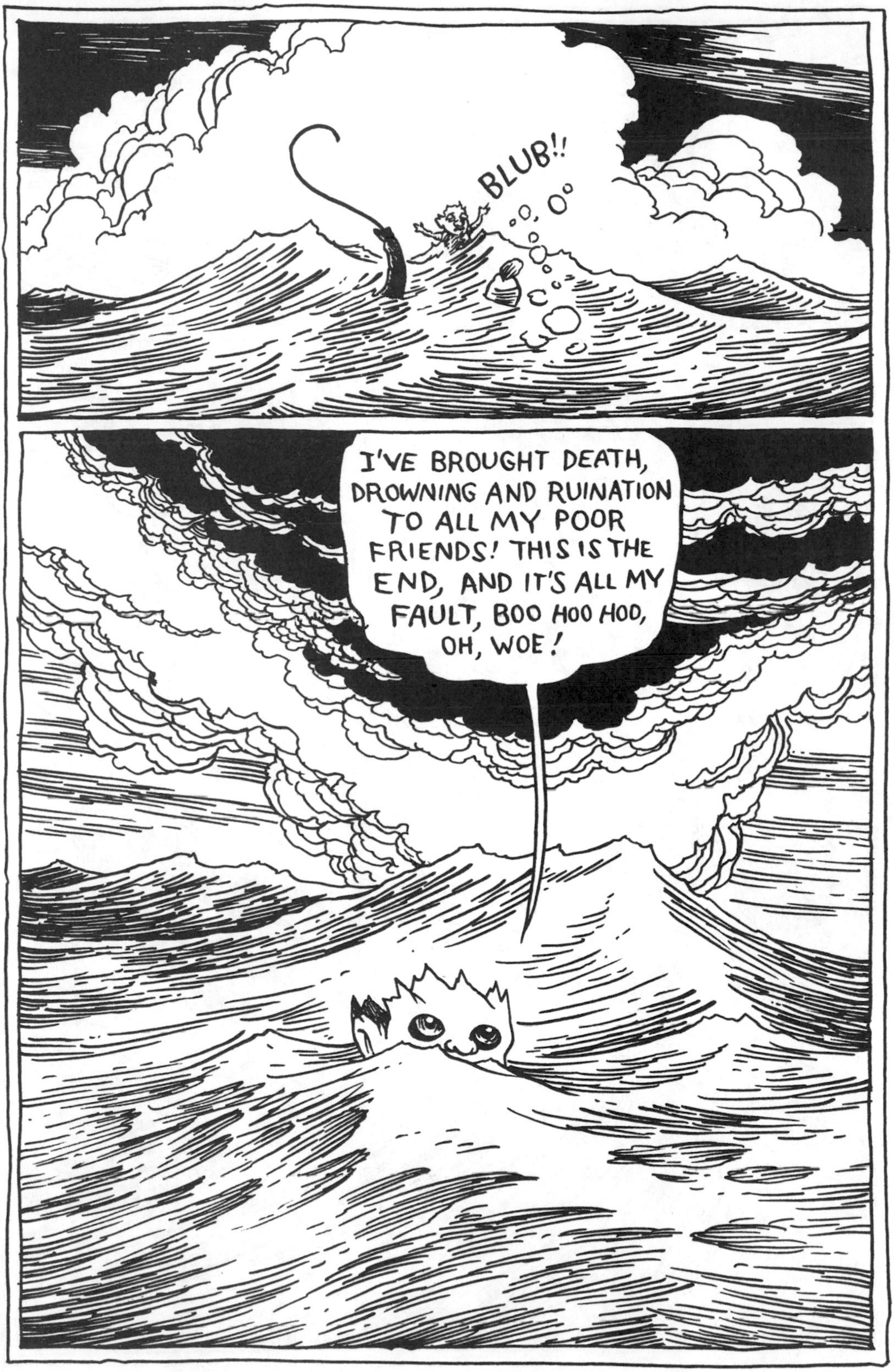
BLUB!!
I'VE BROUGHT DEATH, DROWNING AND RUINATION TO ALL MY POOR FRIENDS! THIS IS THE END, AND IT'S ALL MY FAULT, BOO HOO HOO, OH, WOE!

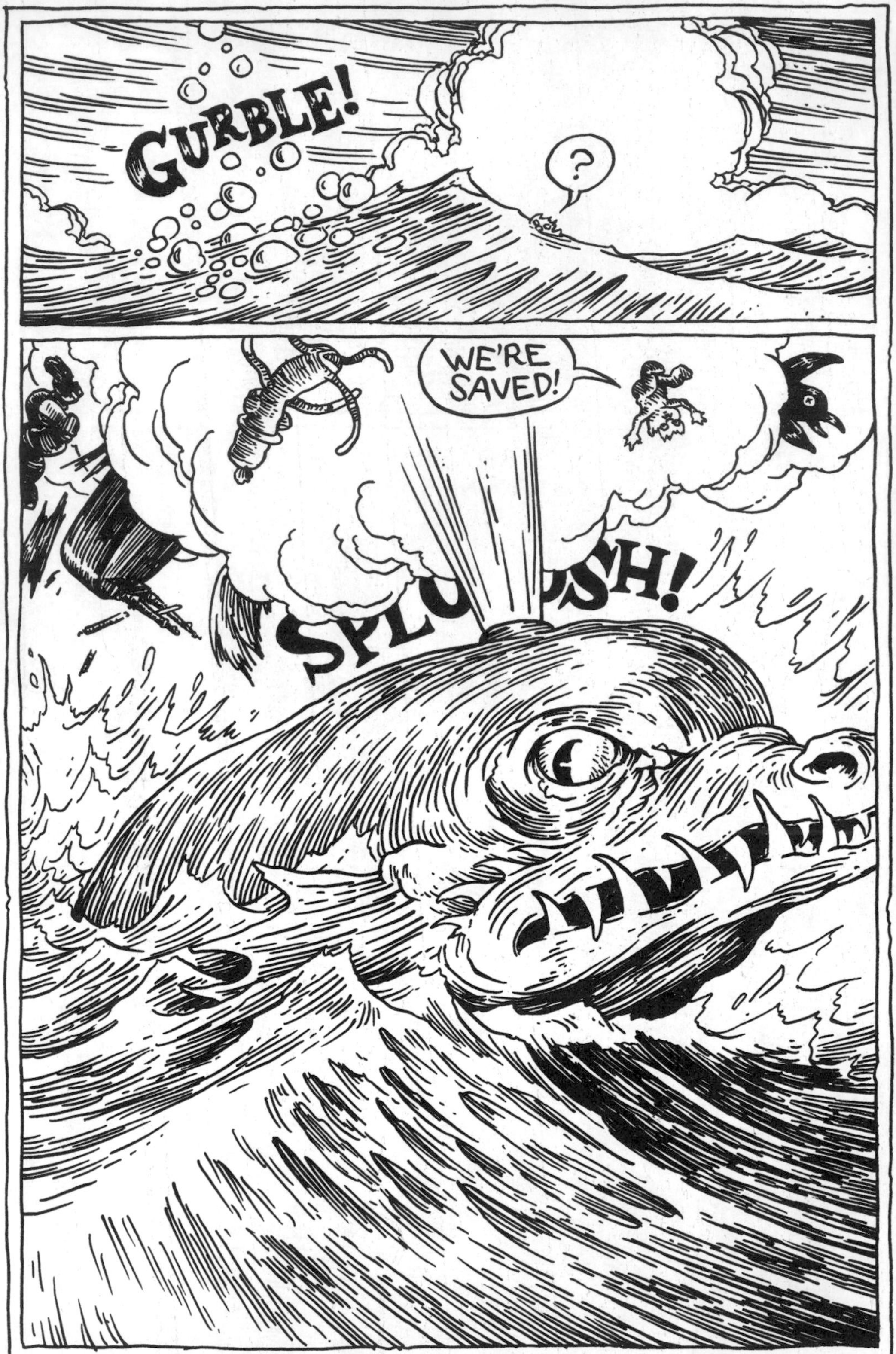
GURBLE!
?
WE'RE SAVED!
SPLU SH!

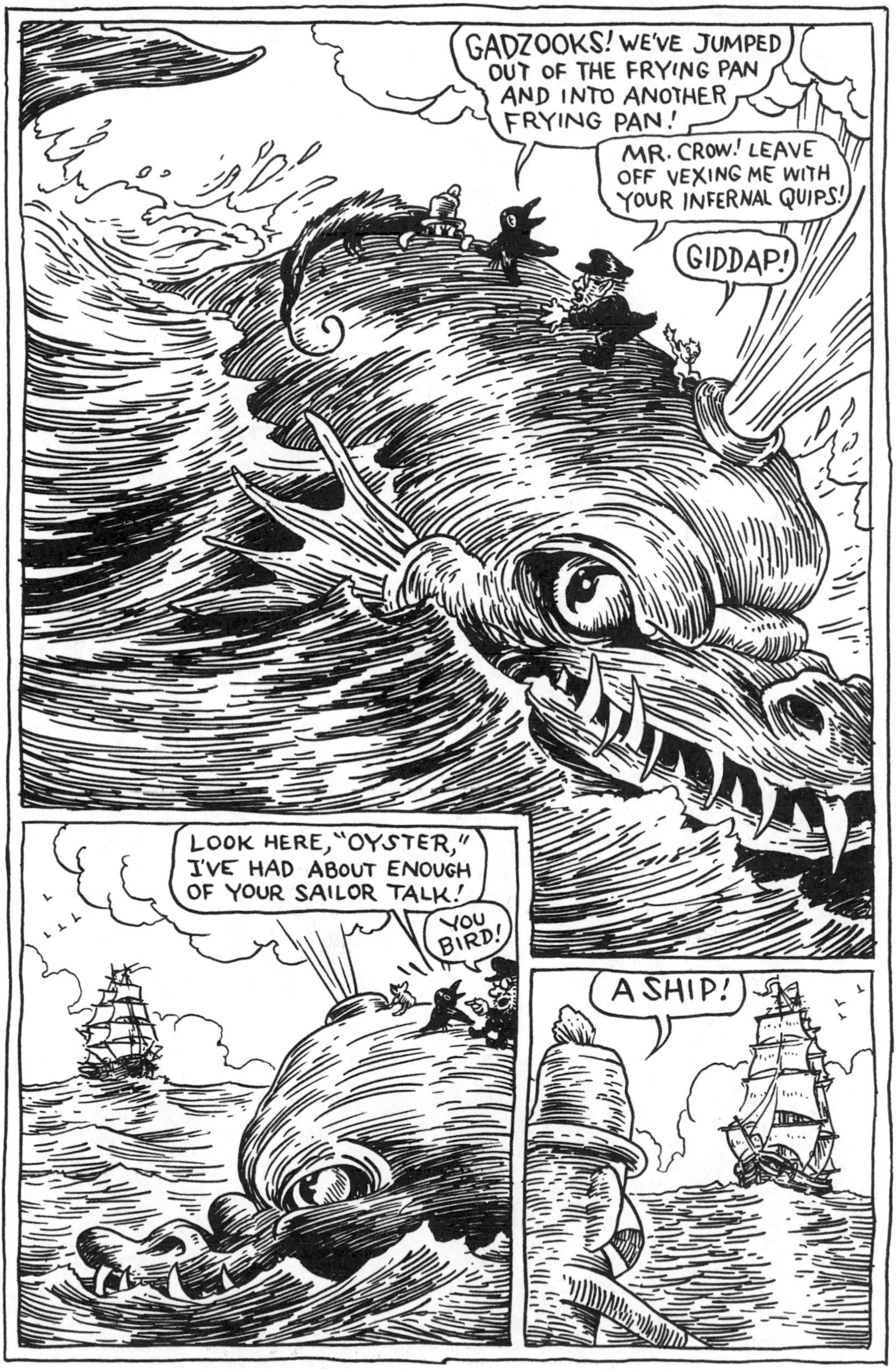
GADZOOKS! WE'VE JUMPED OUT OF THE FRYING PAN AND INTO ANOTHER FRYING PAN!
MR. CROW! LEAVE OFF VEXING ME WITH YOUR INFERNAL QUIPS!
GIDDAP!
LOOK HERE, "OYSTER," I'VE HAD ABOUT ENOUGH OF YOUR SAILOR TALK!
YOU BIRD!
A SHIP!

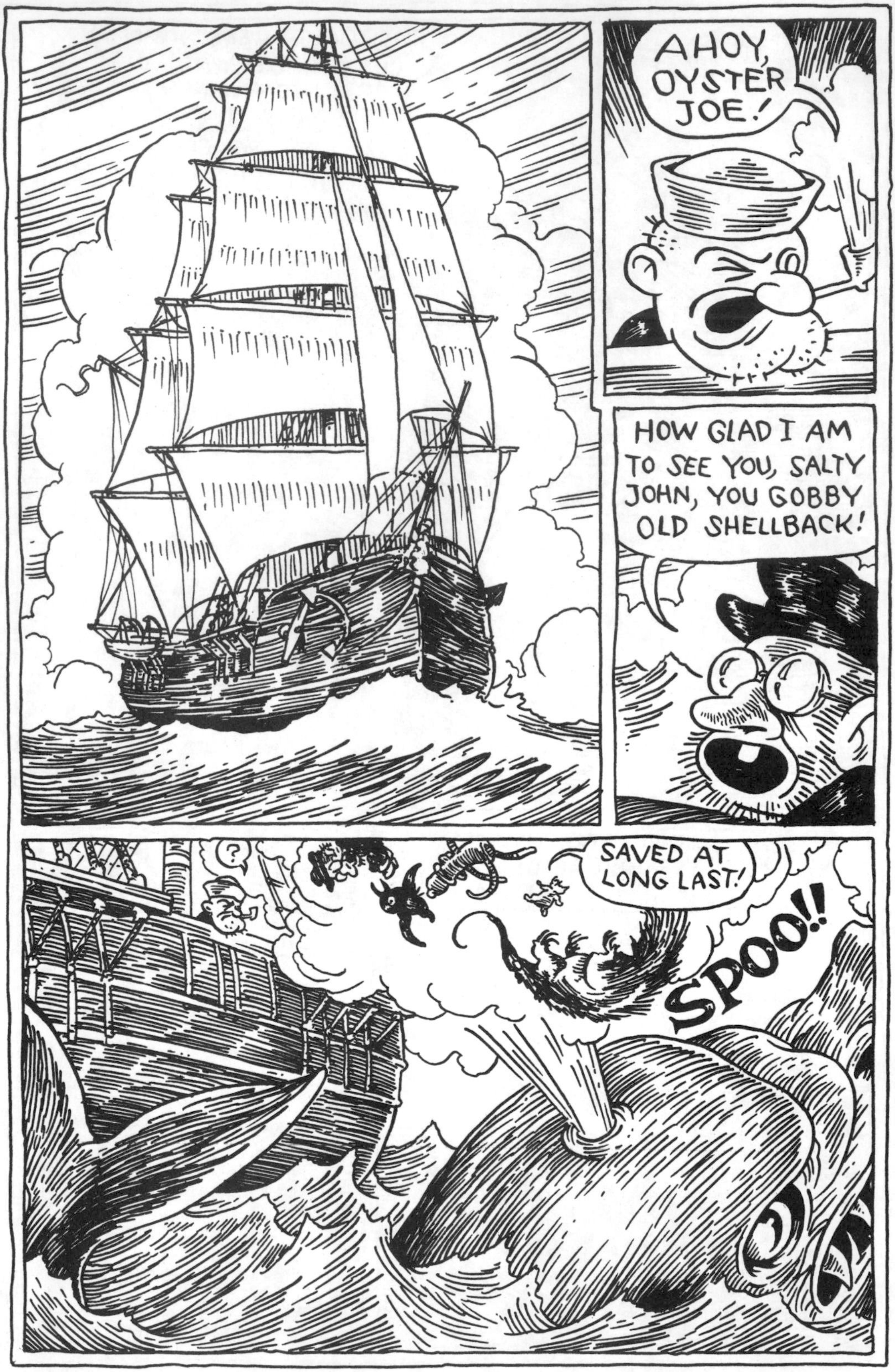
AHOY, OYSTER JOE!
HOW GLAD I AM TO SEE YOU, SALTY JOHN, YOU GOBBY OLD SHELLBACK!
?
SAVED AT LONG LAST!
SPOOO!!

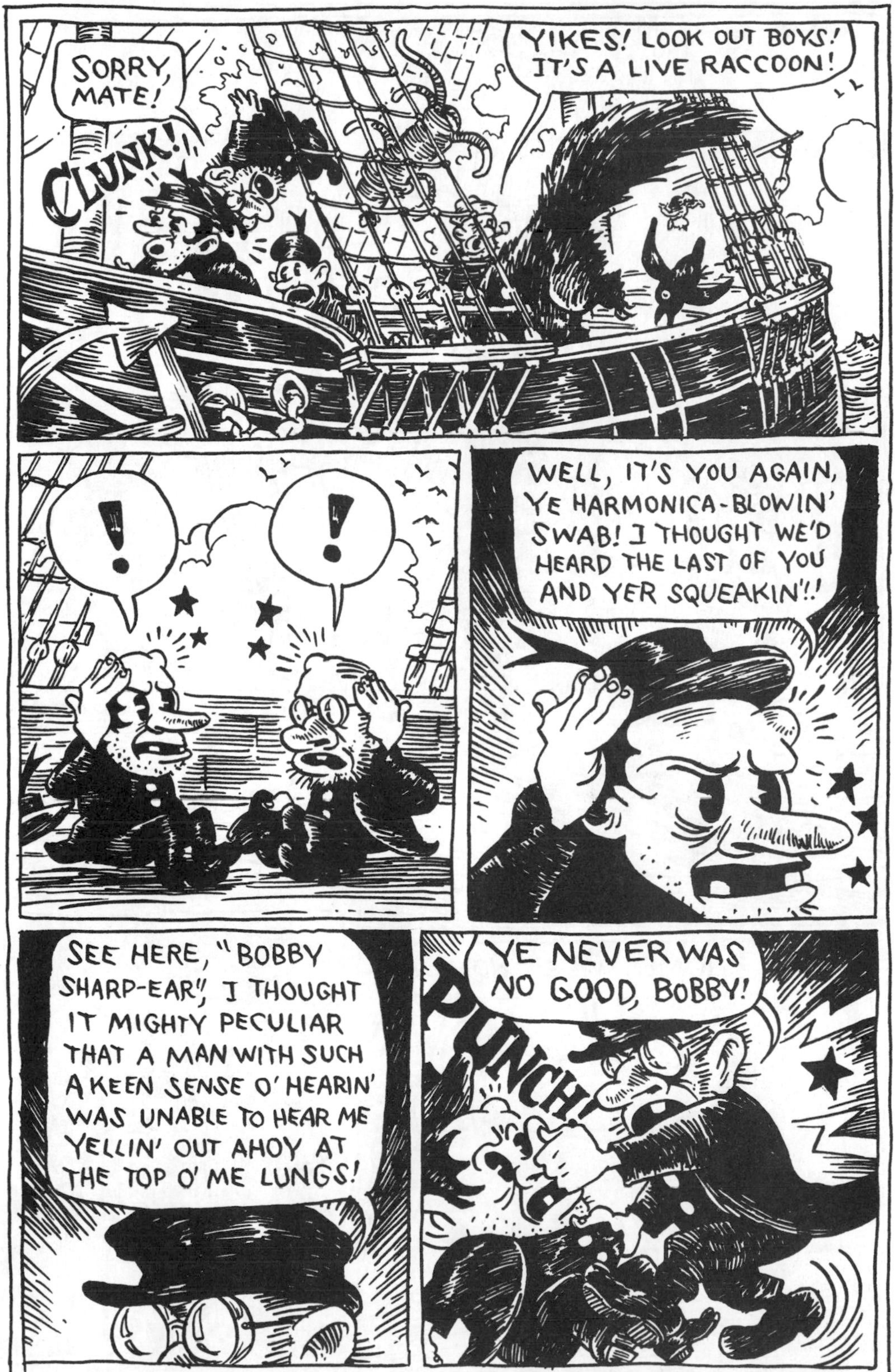
SORRY, MATE!
CLUNK!
YIKES! LOOK OUT BOYS! IT'S A LIVE RACCOON!
!
!
WELL, IT'S YOU AGAIN, YE HARMONICA-BLOWIN' SWAB! I THOUGHT WE'D HEARD THE LAST OF YOU AND YER SQUEAKIN'!!
SEE HERE, "BOBBY SHARP-EAR", I THOUGHT IT MIGHTY PECULIAR THAT A MAN WITH SUCH A KEEN SENSE O' HEARIN' WAS UNABLE TO HEAR ME YELLIN' OUT AHOY AT THE TOP O' ME LUNGS!
YE NEVER WAS NO GOOD, BOBBY!
PUNCH!

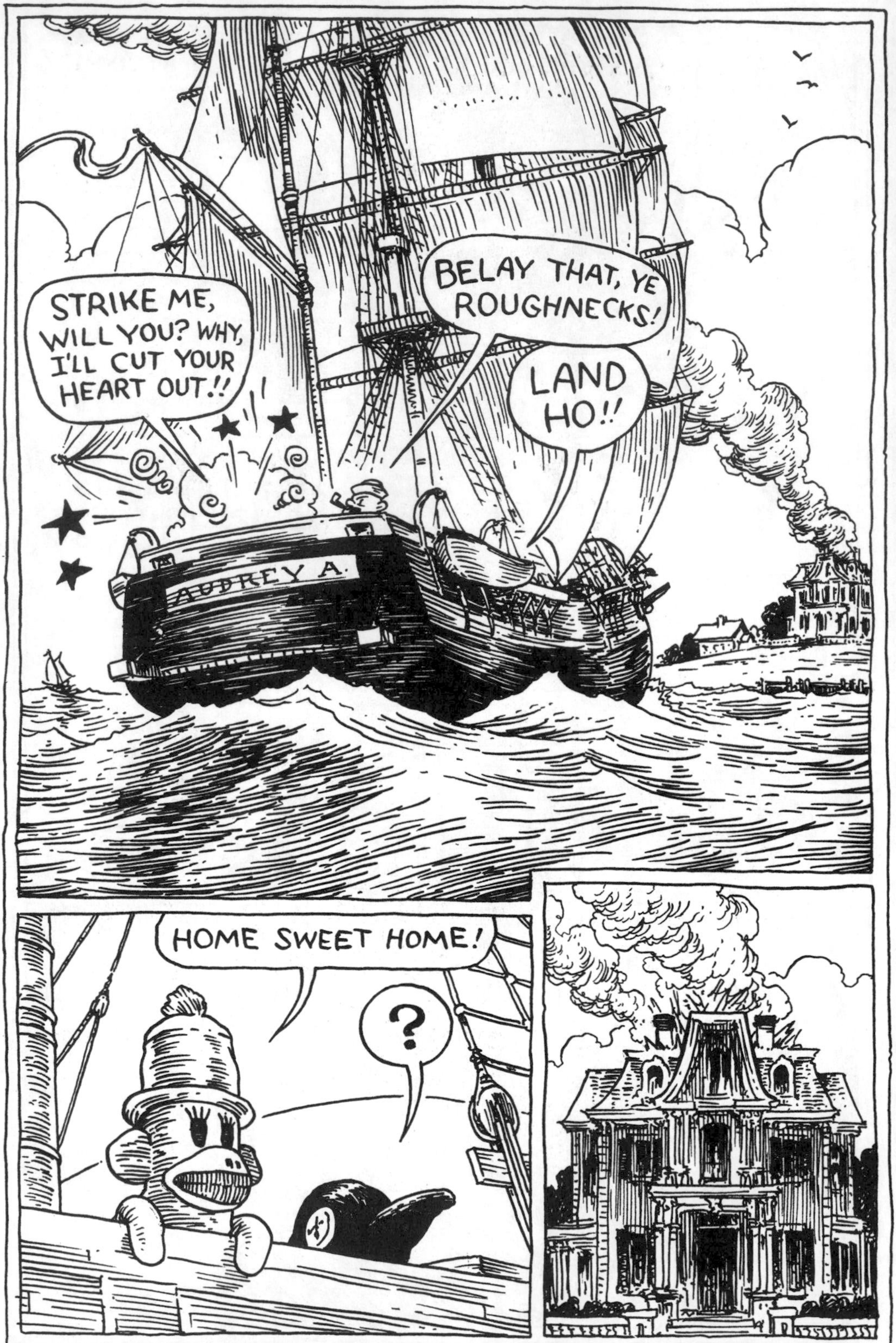
STRIKE ME, WILL YOU? WHY, I'LL CUT YOUR HEART OUT!!
BELAY THAT, YE ROUGHNECKS!
LAND HO!!
AUDREY A.
HOME SWEET HOME!
?

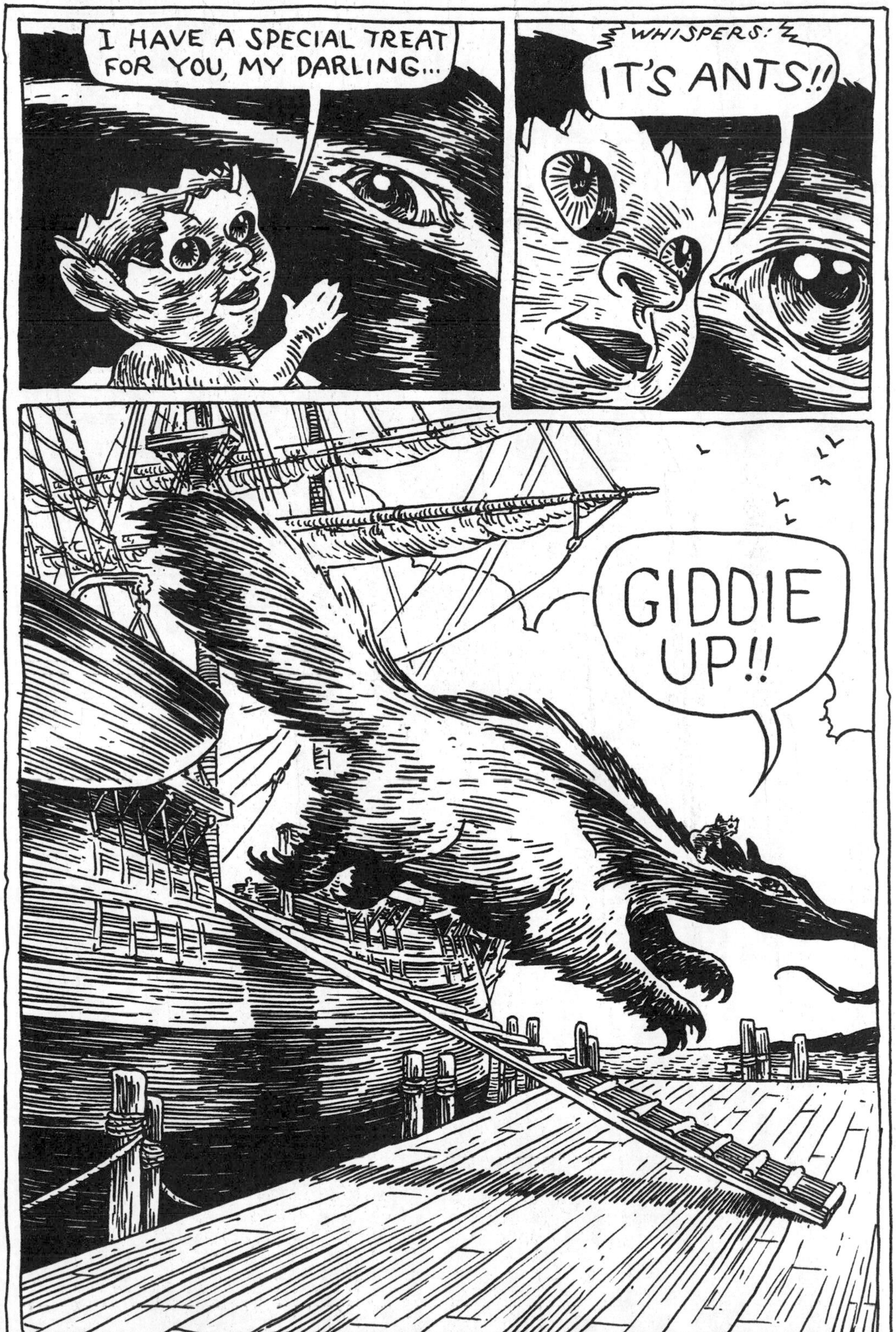
I HAVE A SPECIAL TREAT FOR YOU, MY DARLING...
WHISPERS:
IT'S ANTS!!
GIDDIE UP!!

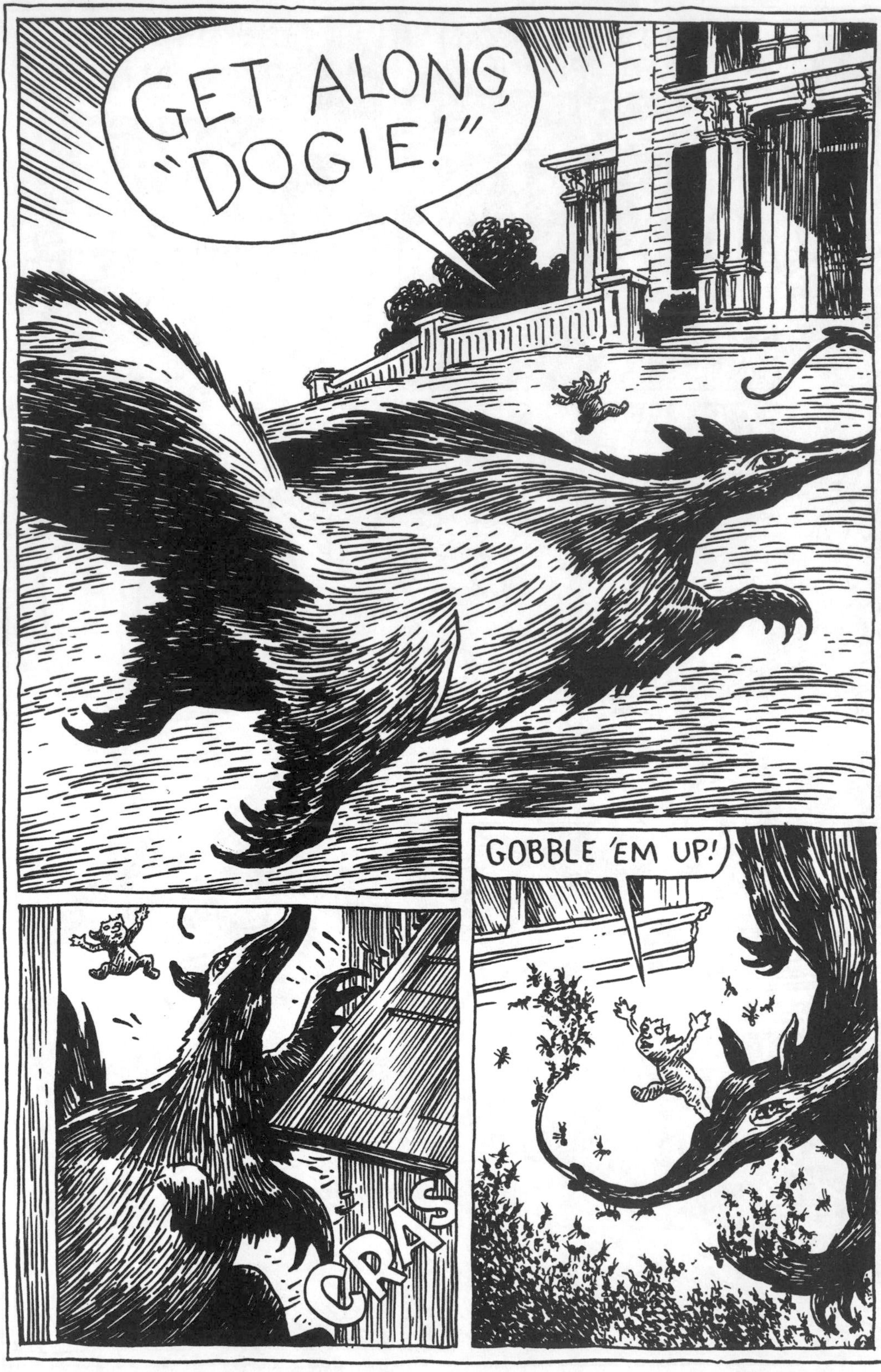
GET ALONG, "DOGIE!"
GOBBLE 'EM UP!
CRAS

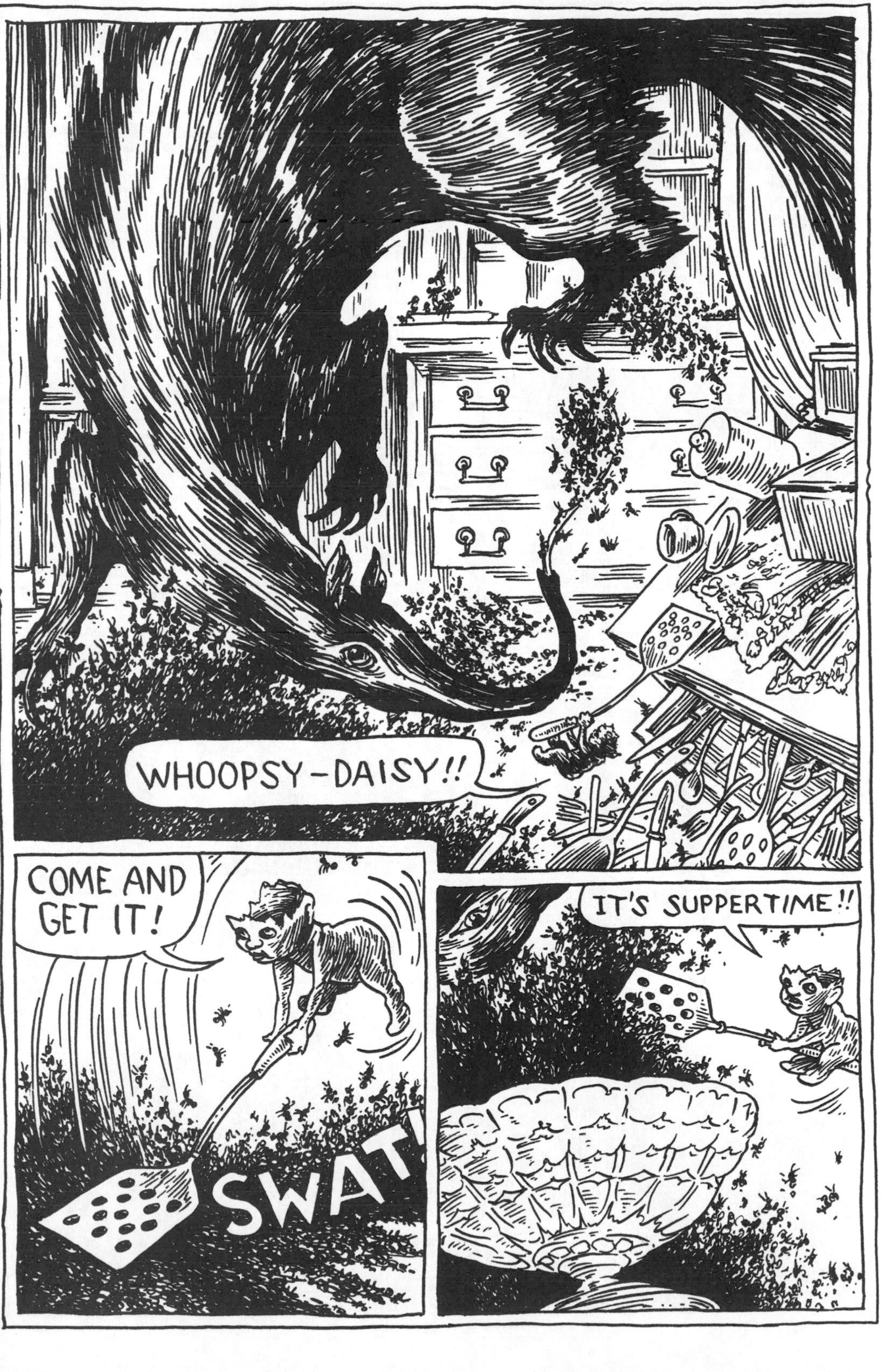
WHOOPSY-DAISY!!
COME AND GET IT!
SWAT!
IT'S SUPPERTIME!!

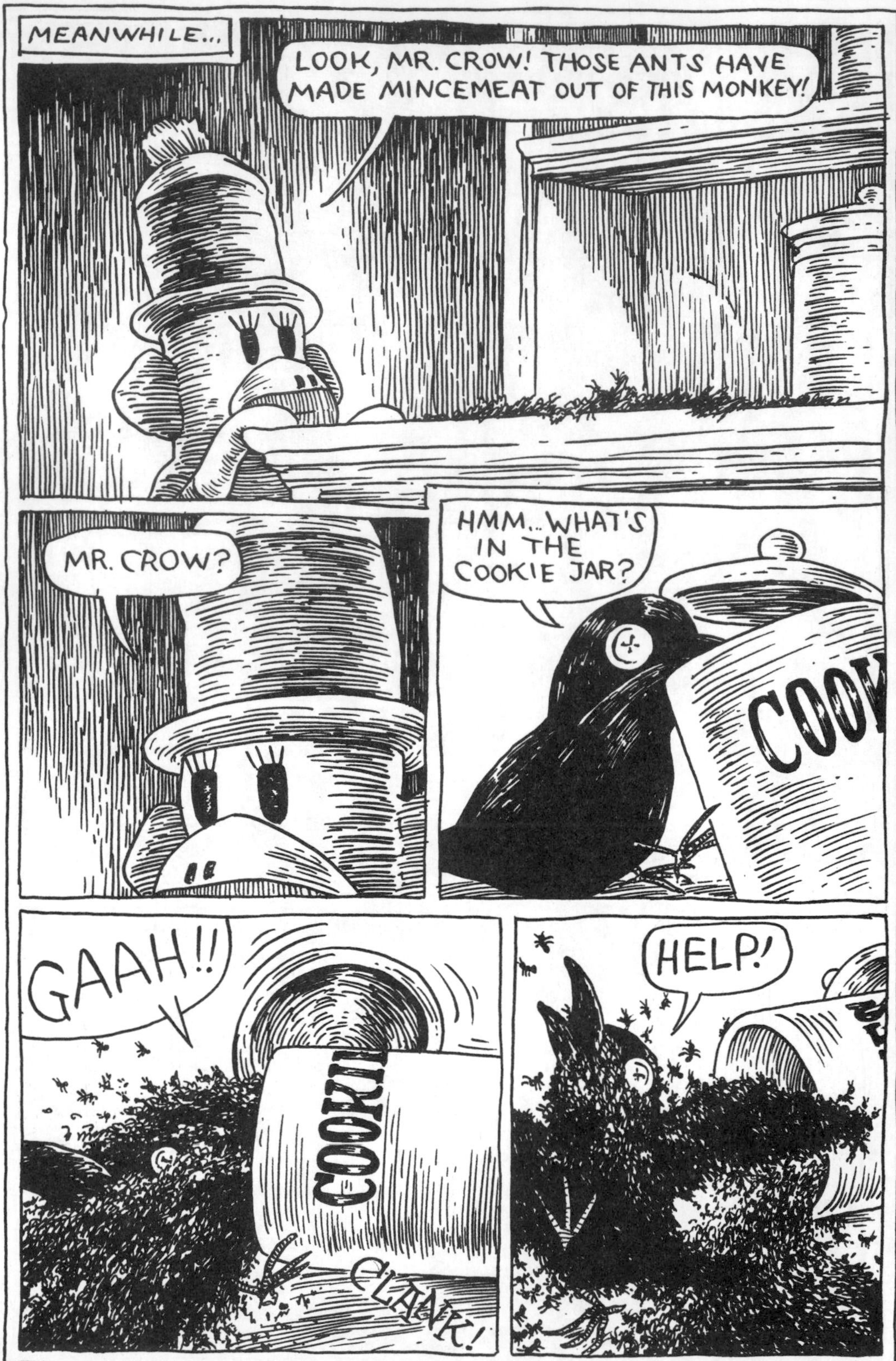
MEANWHILE...
LOOK, MR. CROW! THOSE ANTS HAVE MADE MINCEMEAT OUT OF THIS MONKEY!
MR. CROW?
HMM.. WHAT'S IN THE COOKIE JAR?
GAAH!!
CLANK!
HELP!

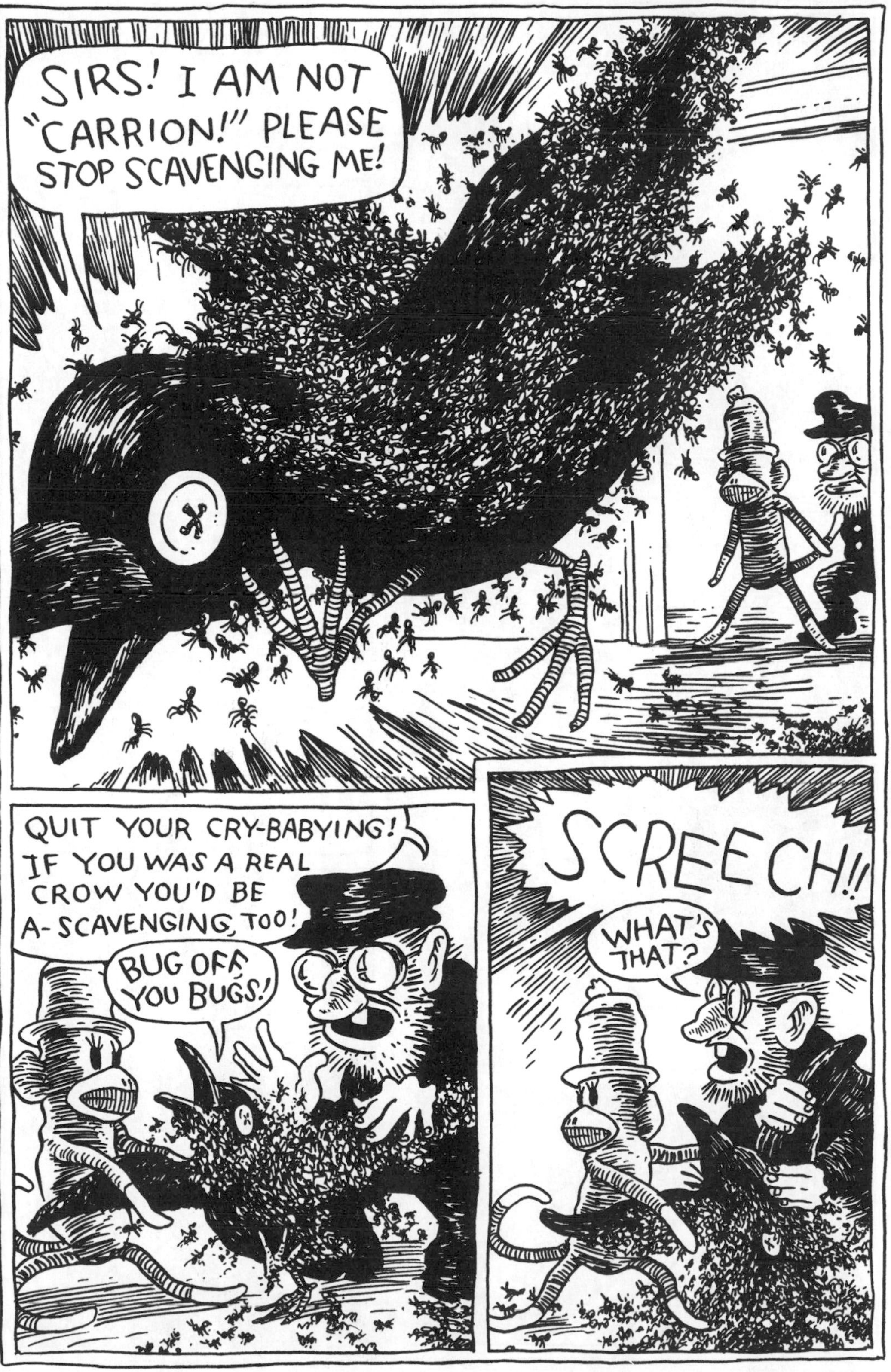
SIRS! I AM NOT "CARRION!" PLEASE STOP SCAVENGING ME!
QUIT YOUR CRY-BABYING! IF YOU WAS A REAL CROW YOU'D BE A-SCAVENGING, TOO!
BUG OFF, YOU BUGS!
SCREECH!!
WHAT'S THAT?

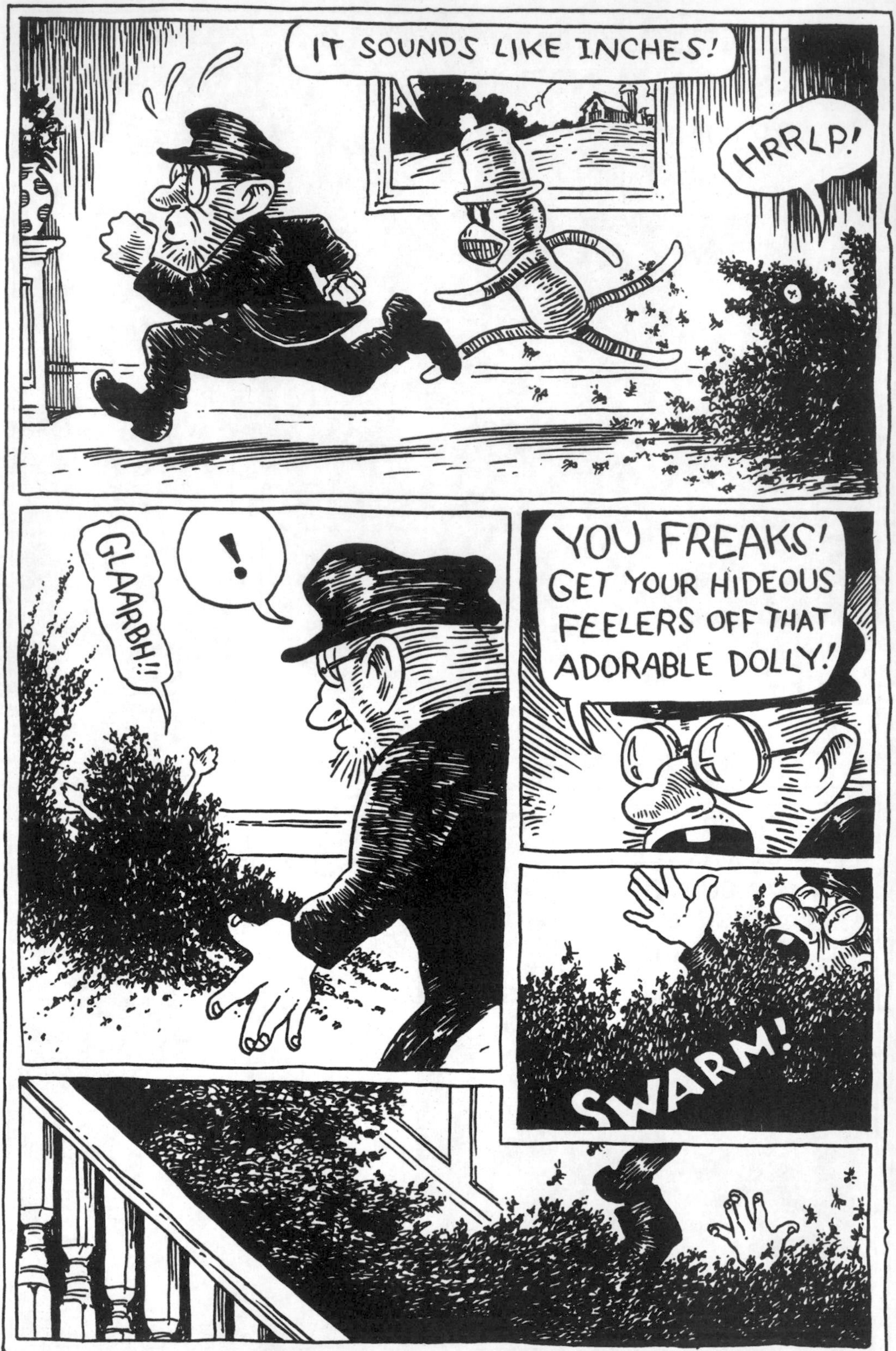
IT SOUNDS LIKE INCHES!
HRRLP!
GLAARBH!!
!
YOU FREAKS! GET YOUR HIDEOUS FEELERS OFF THAT ADORABLE DOLLY!
SWARM!

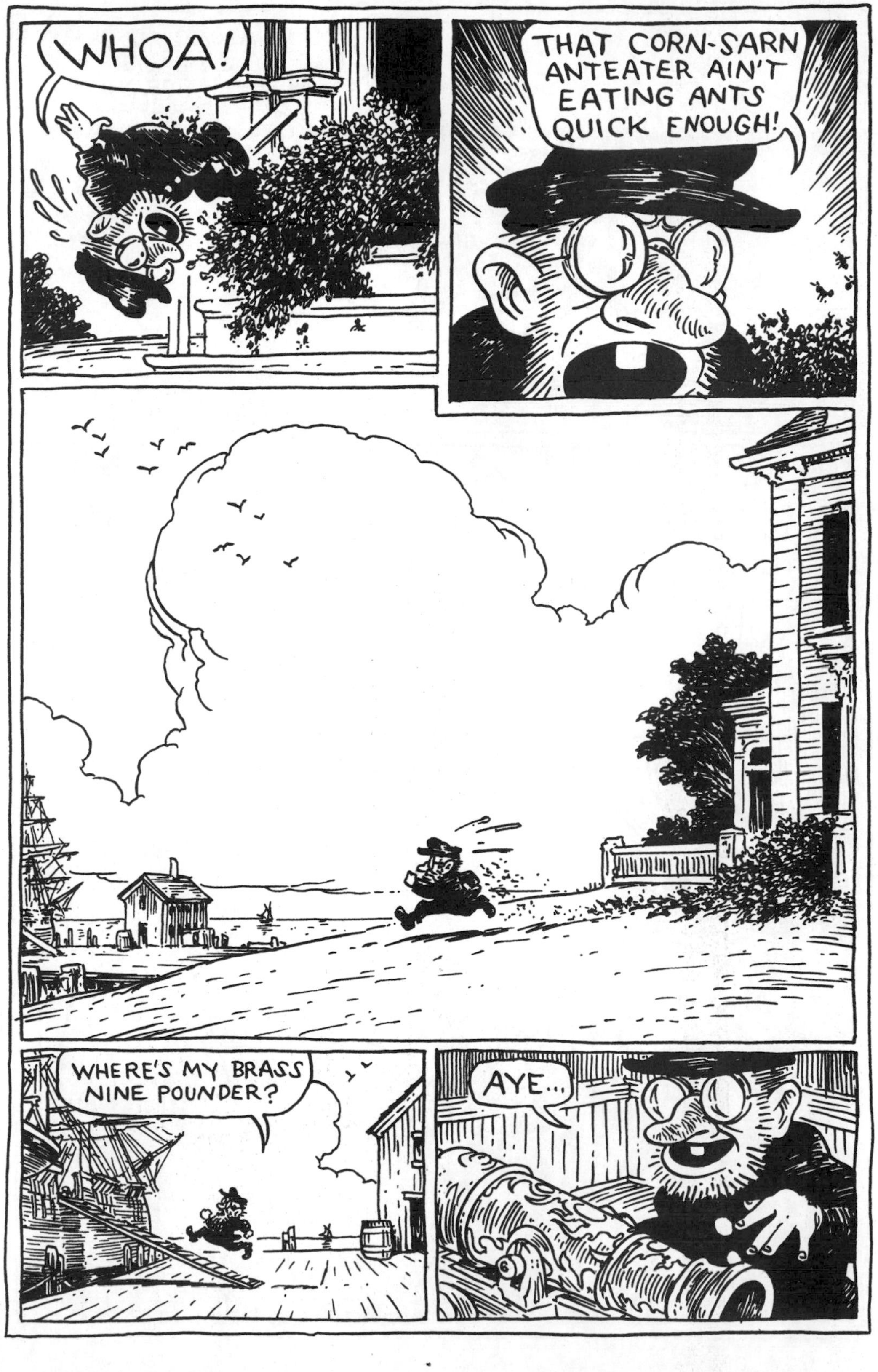
WHOA!
THAT CORN-SARN ANTEATER AIN'T EATING ANTS QUICK ENOUGH!
WHERE'S MY BRASS NINE POUNDER?
AYE...

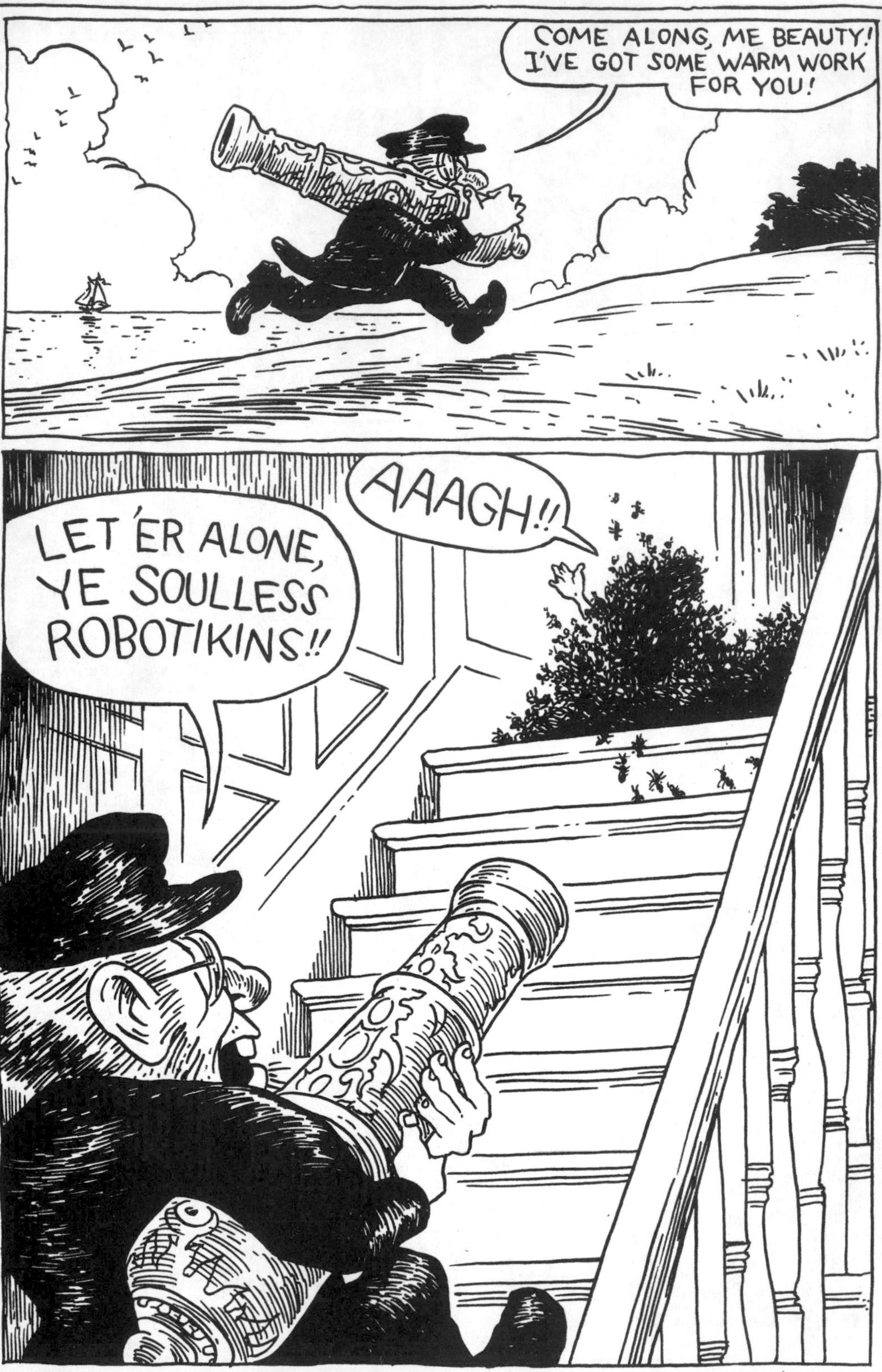
COME ALONG, ME BEAUTY! I'VE GOT SOME WARM WORK FOR YOU!
LET 'ER ALONE, YE SOULLESS ROBOTIKINS!!
AAAGH!!

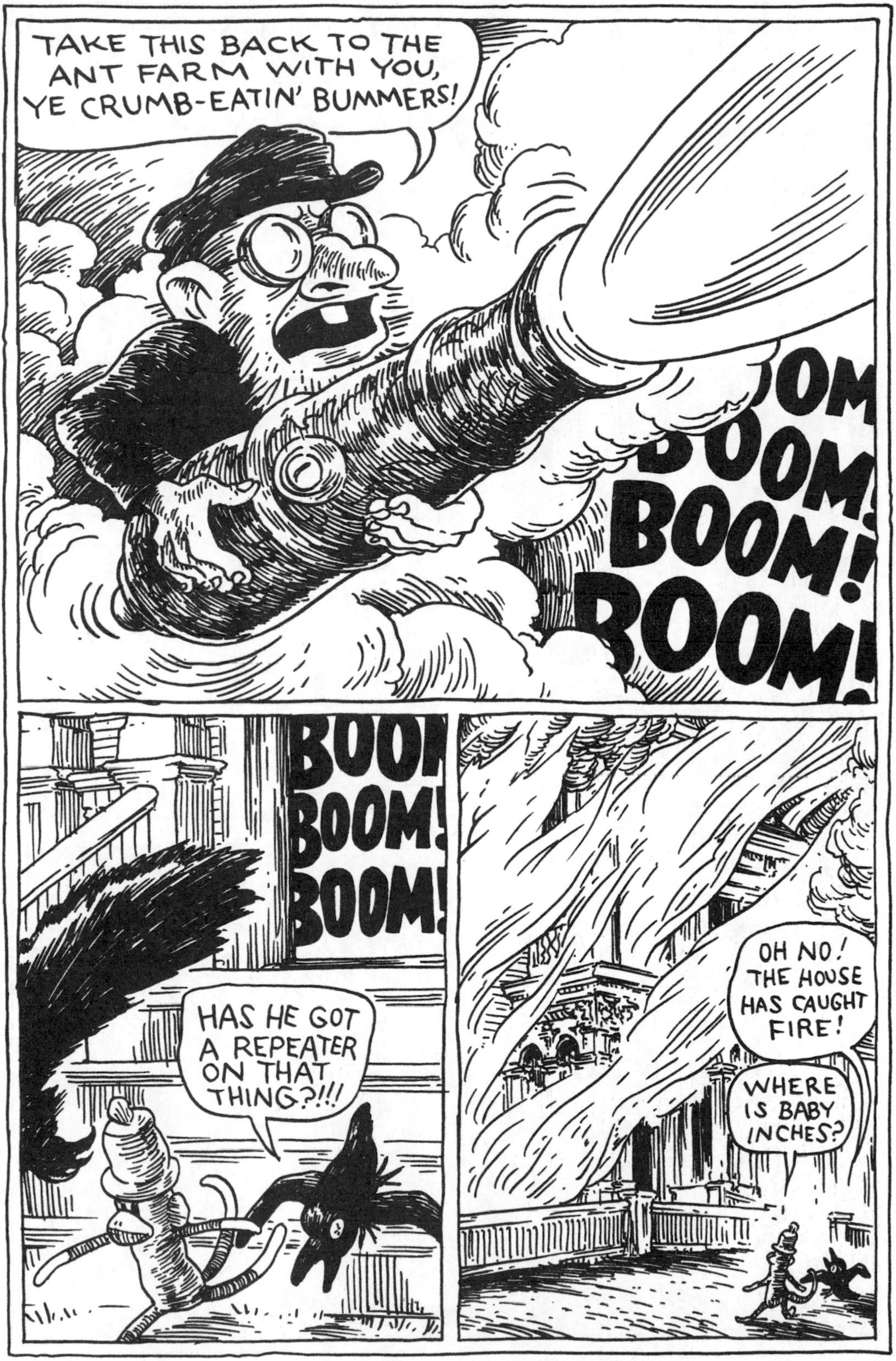
TAKE THIS BACK TO THE ANT FARM WITH YOU, YE CRUMB-EATIN' BUMMERS!
BOOM! BOOM! BOOM!
BOOM! BOOM!
HAS HE GOT A REPEATER ON THAT THING?!!!
OH NO! THE HOUSE HAS CAUGHT FIRE!
WHERE IS BABY INCHES?

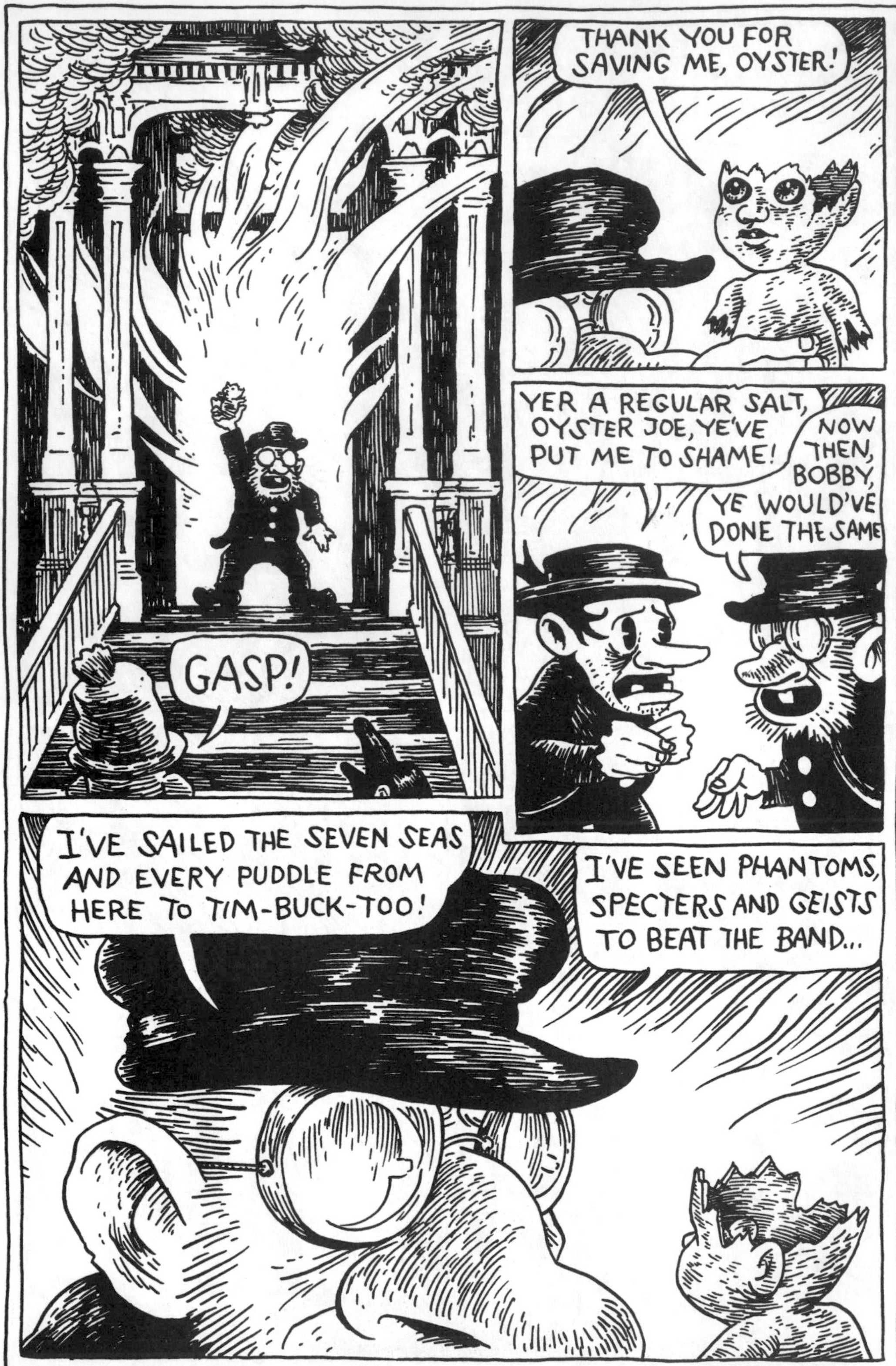
GASP!
THANK YOU FOR SAVING ME, OYSTER!
YER A REGULAR SALT, OYSTER JOE, YE'VE PUT ME TO SHAME!
NOW THEN, BOBBY, YE WOULD'VE DONE THE SAME
I'VE SAILED THE SEVEN SEAS AND EVERY PUDDLE FROM HERE TO TIM-BUCK-TOO!
I'VE SEEN PHANTOMS, SPECTERS AND GEISTS TO BEAT THE BAND...

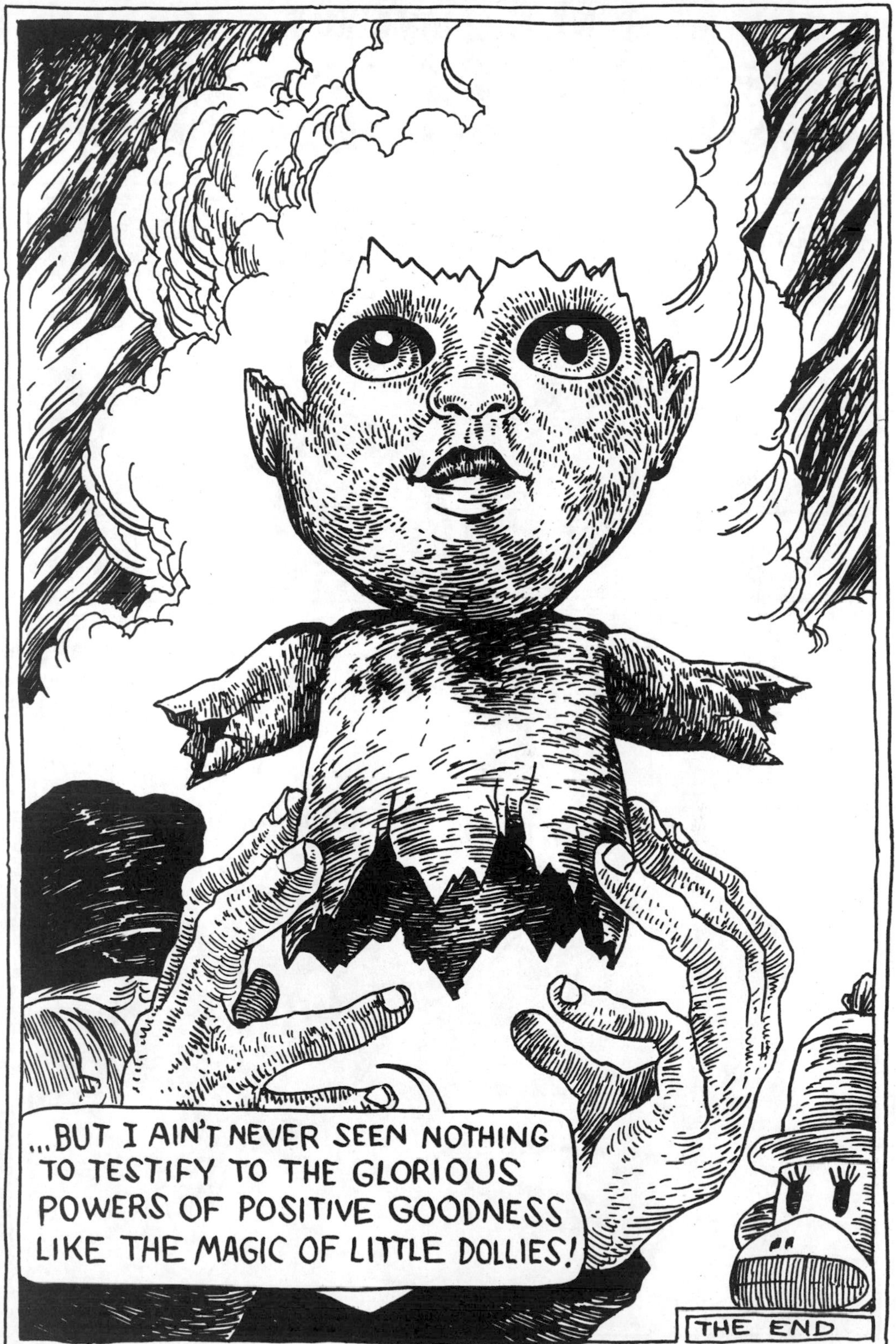
...BUT I AIN'T NEVER SEEN NOTHING TO TESTIFY TO THE GLORIOUS POWERS OF POSITIVE GOODNESS LIKE THE MAGIC OF LITTLE DOLLIES!
THE END

TONY MILLIONAIRE's

SOCK MONKEY™

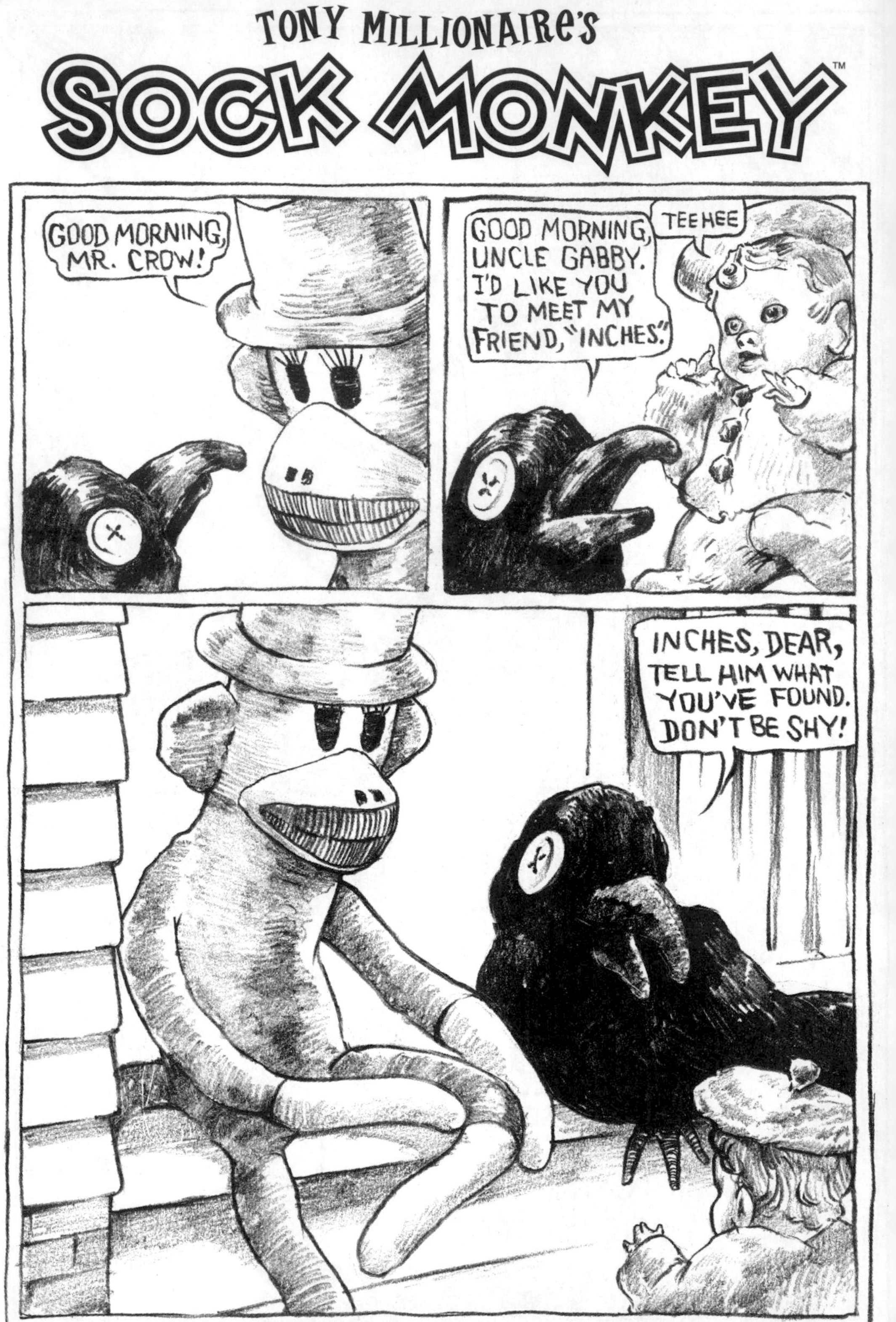
GOOD MORNING, MR. CROW!
GOOD MORNING, UNCLE GABBY. I'D LIKE YOU TO MEET MY FRIEND, "INCHES."
TEE HEE
INCHES, DEAR, TELL HIM WHAT YOU'VE FOUND. DON'T BE SHY!

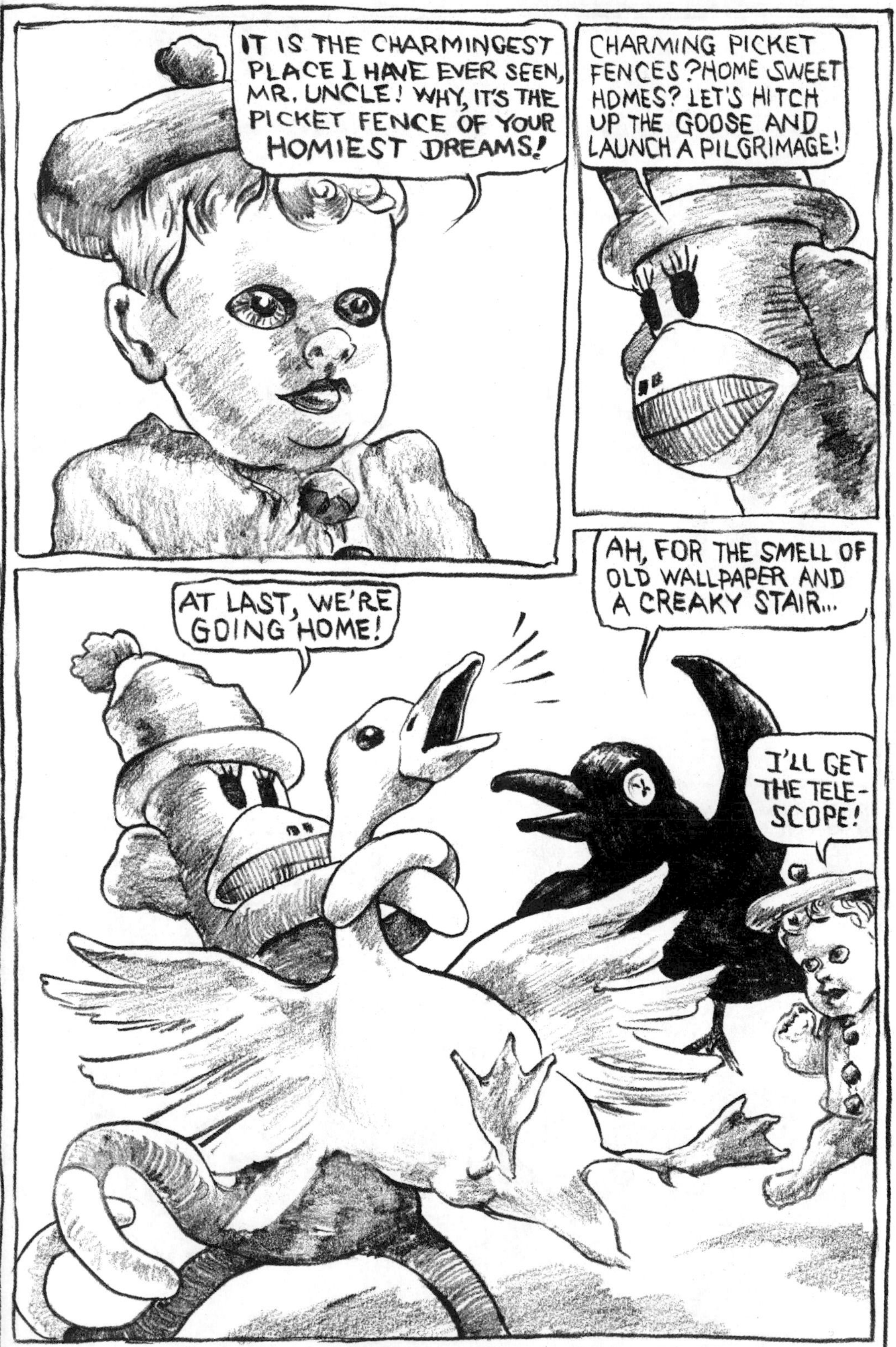
IT IS THE CHARMINGEST PLACE I HAVE EVER SEEN, MR. UNCLE! WHY, IT'S THE PICKET FENCE OF YOUR HOMIEST DREAMS!
CHARMING PICKET FENCES? HOME SWEET HOMES? LET'S HITCH UP THE GOOSE AND LAUNCH A PILGRIMAGE!
AT LAST, WE'RE GOING HOME!
AH, FOR THE SMELL OF OLD WALLPAPER AND A CREAKY STAIR...
I'LL GET THE TELE-SCOPE!

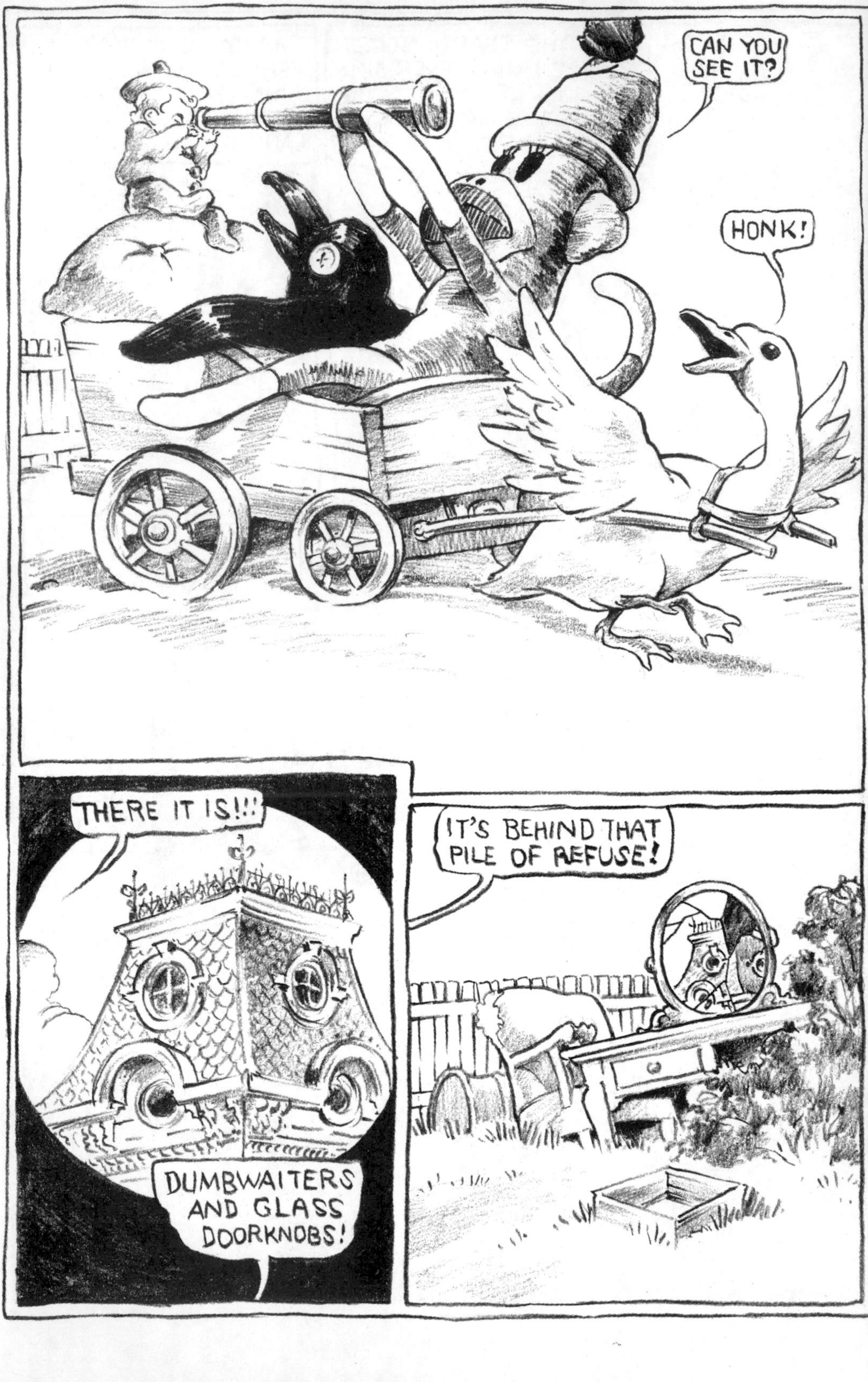
CAN YOU SEE IT?
HONK!
THERE IT IS!!!
DUMBWAITERS AND GLASS DOORKNOBS!
IT'S BEHIND THAT PILE OF REFUSE!

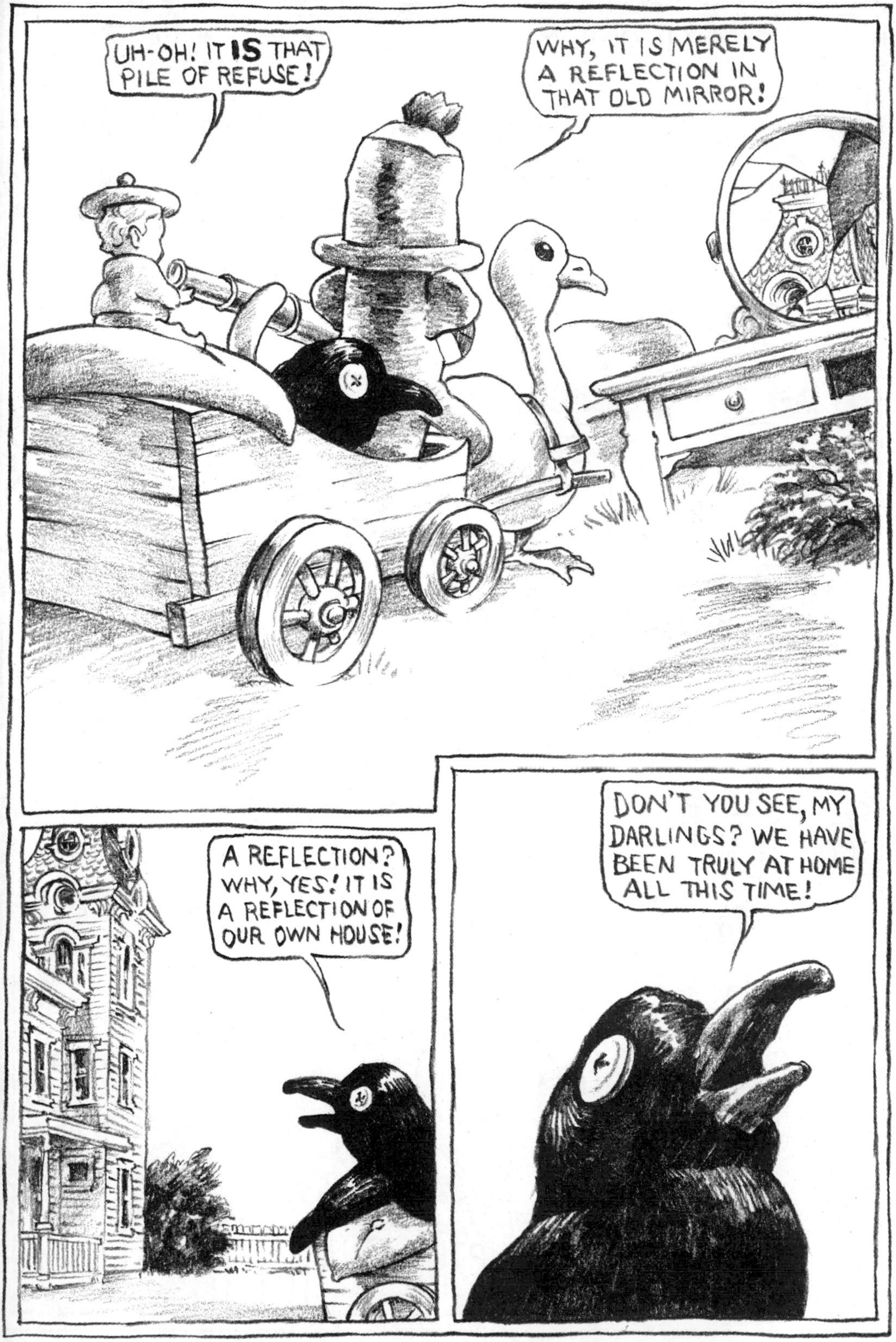
UH-OH! IT IS THAT PILE OF REFUSE!
WHY, IT IS MERELY A REFLECTION IN THAT OLD MIRROR!
A REFLECTION? WHY, YES! IT IS A REFLECTION OF OUR OWN HOUSE!
DON'T YOU SEE, MY DARLINGS? WE HAVE BEEN TRULY AT HOME ALL THIS TIME!

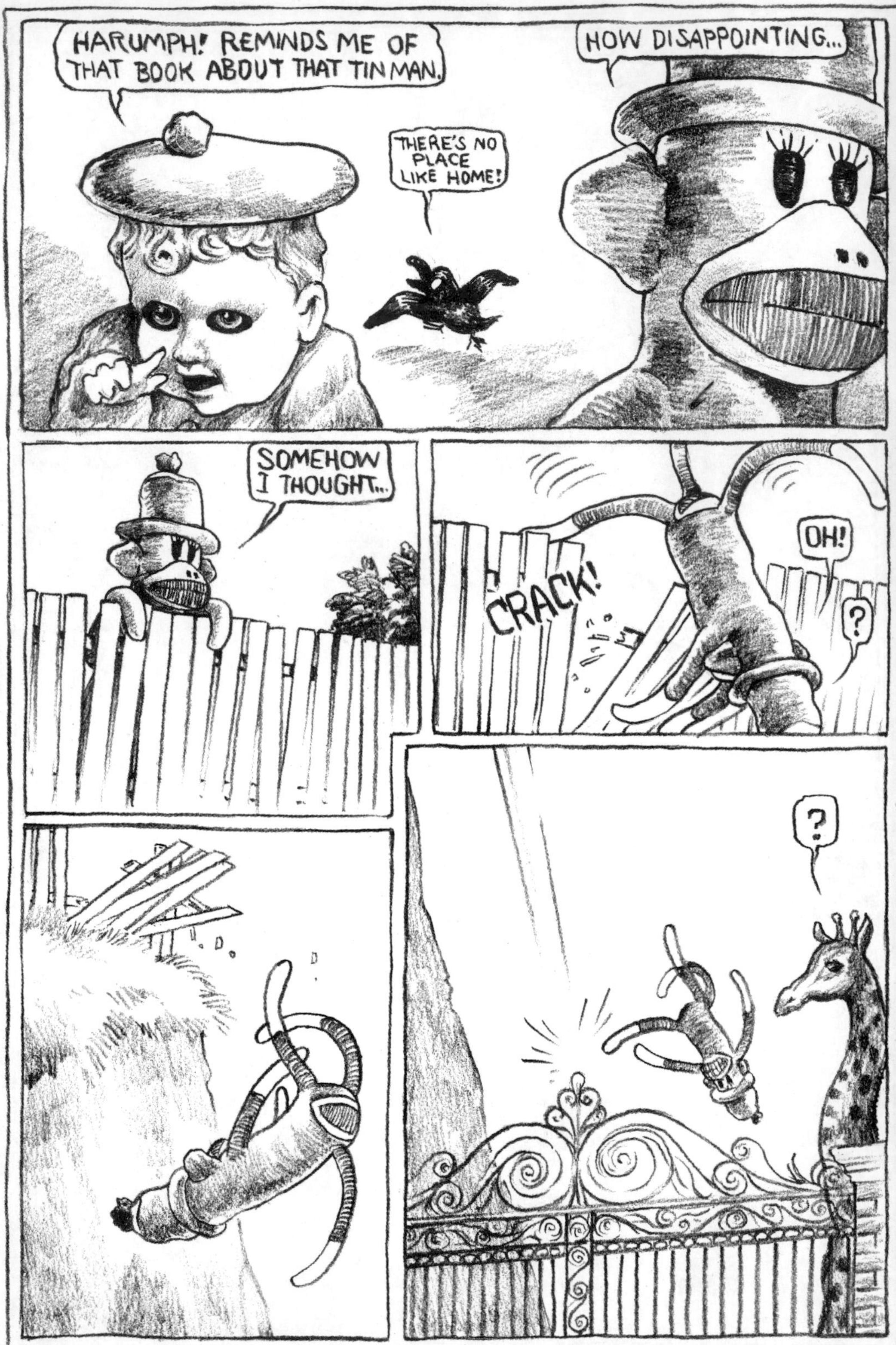
HARUMPH! REMINDS ME OF THAT BOOK ABOUT THAT TIN MAN.
THERE'S NO PLACE LIKE HOME!
HOW DISAPPOINTING...
SOMEHOW I THOUGHT...
CRACK!
OH!
?
?

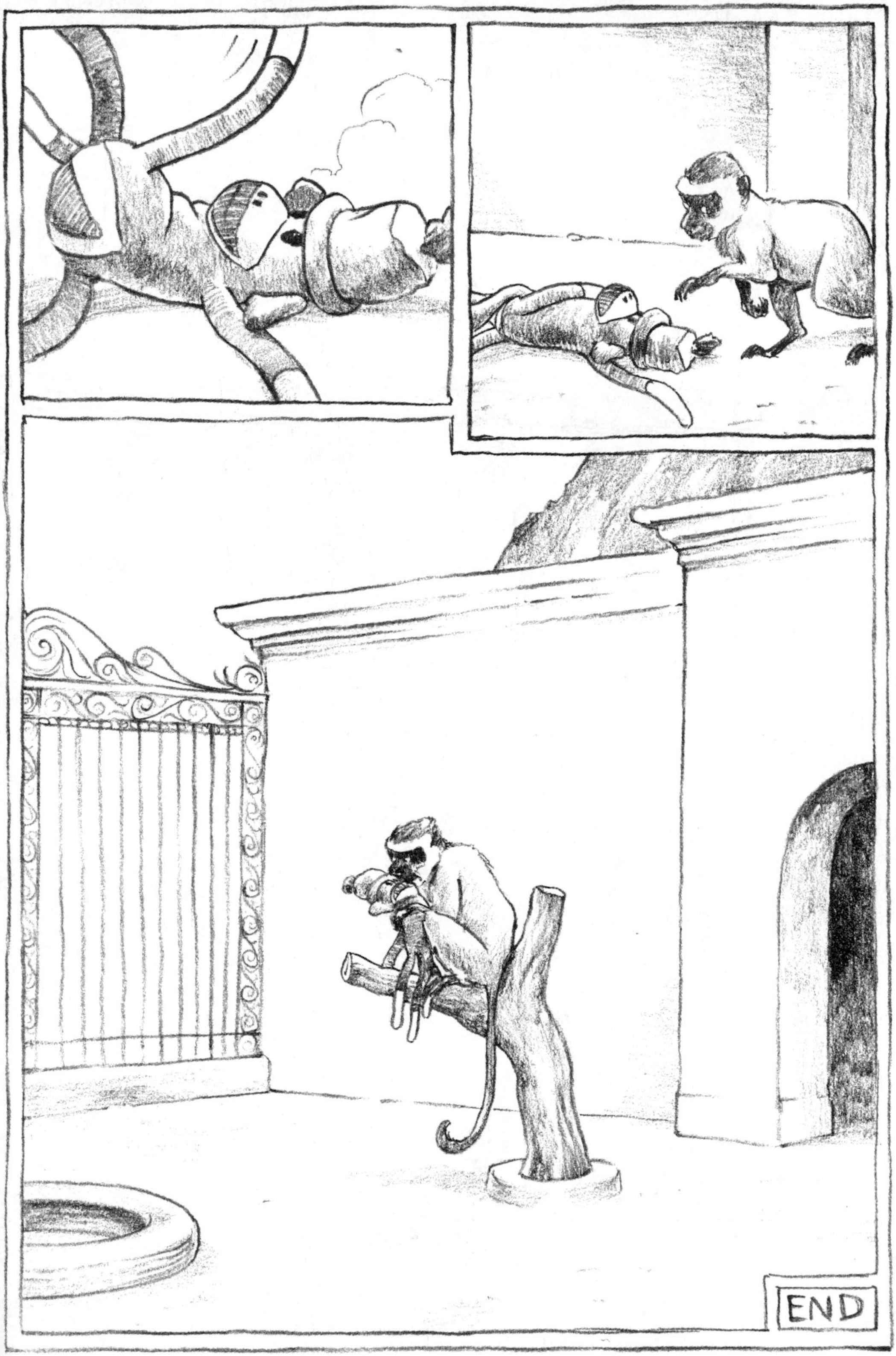
END

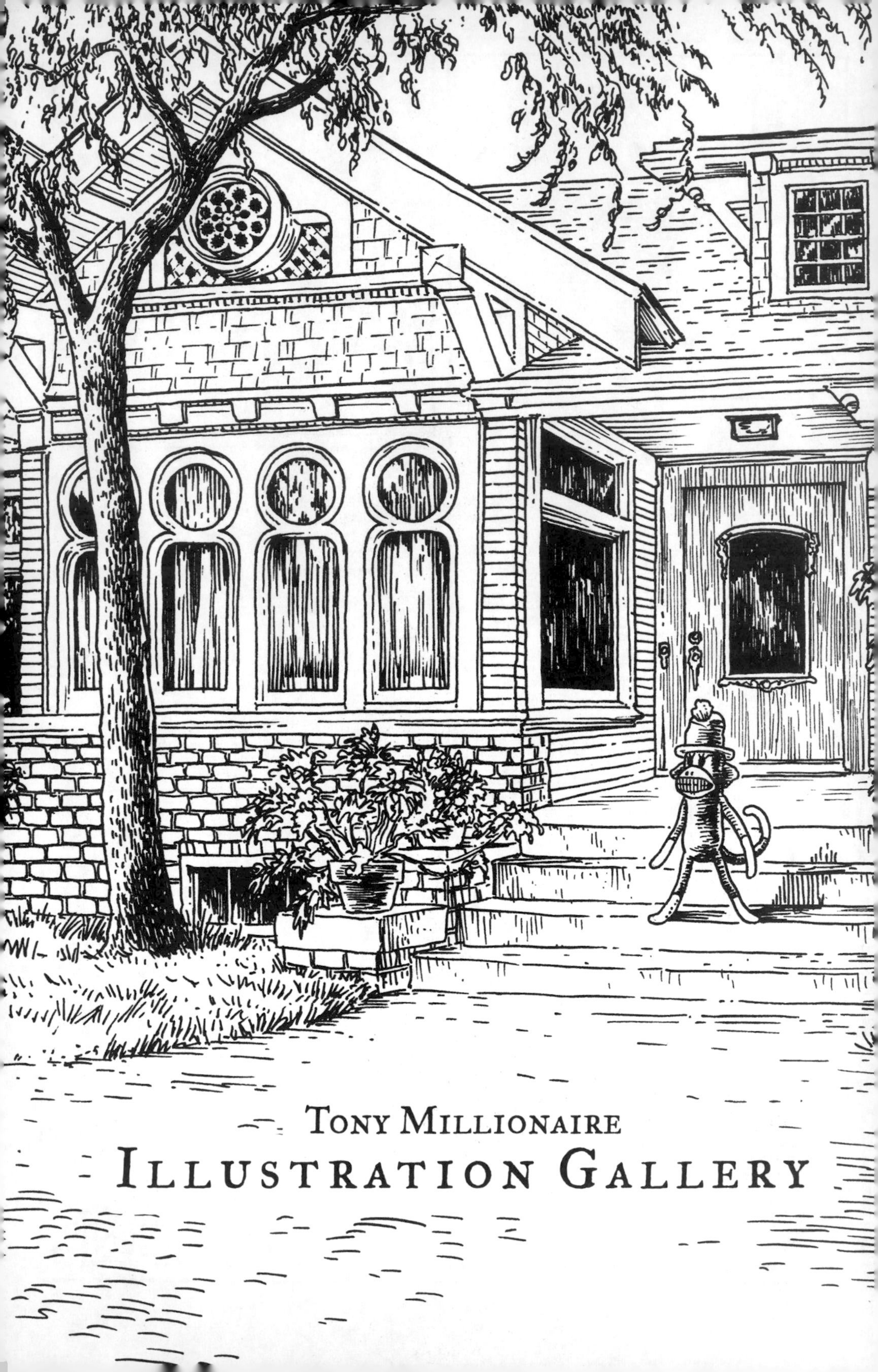

Tony Millionaire

Illustration Gallery

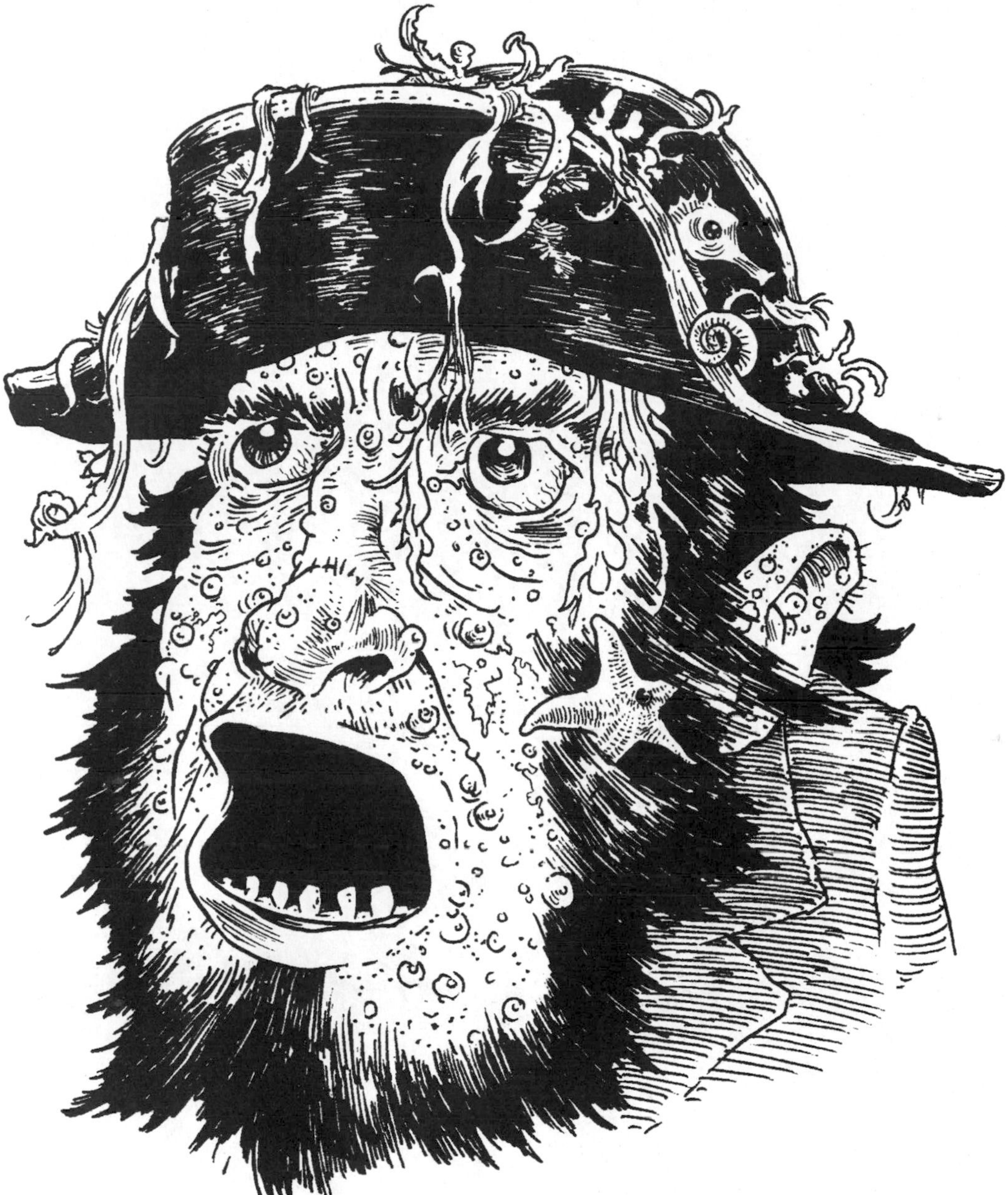

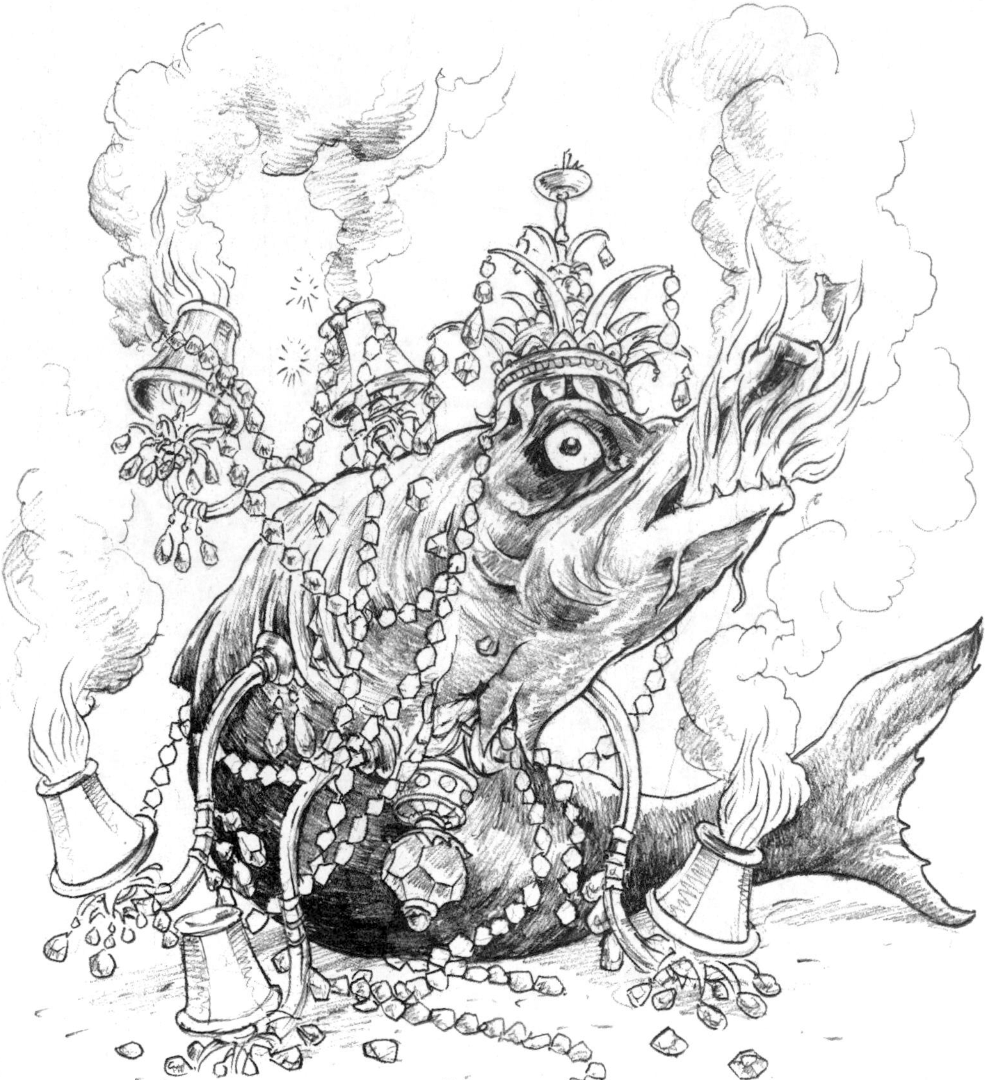

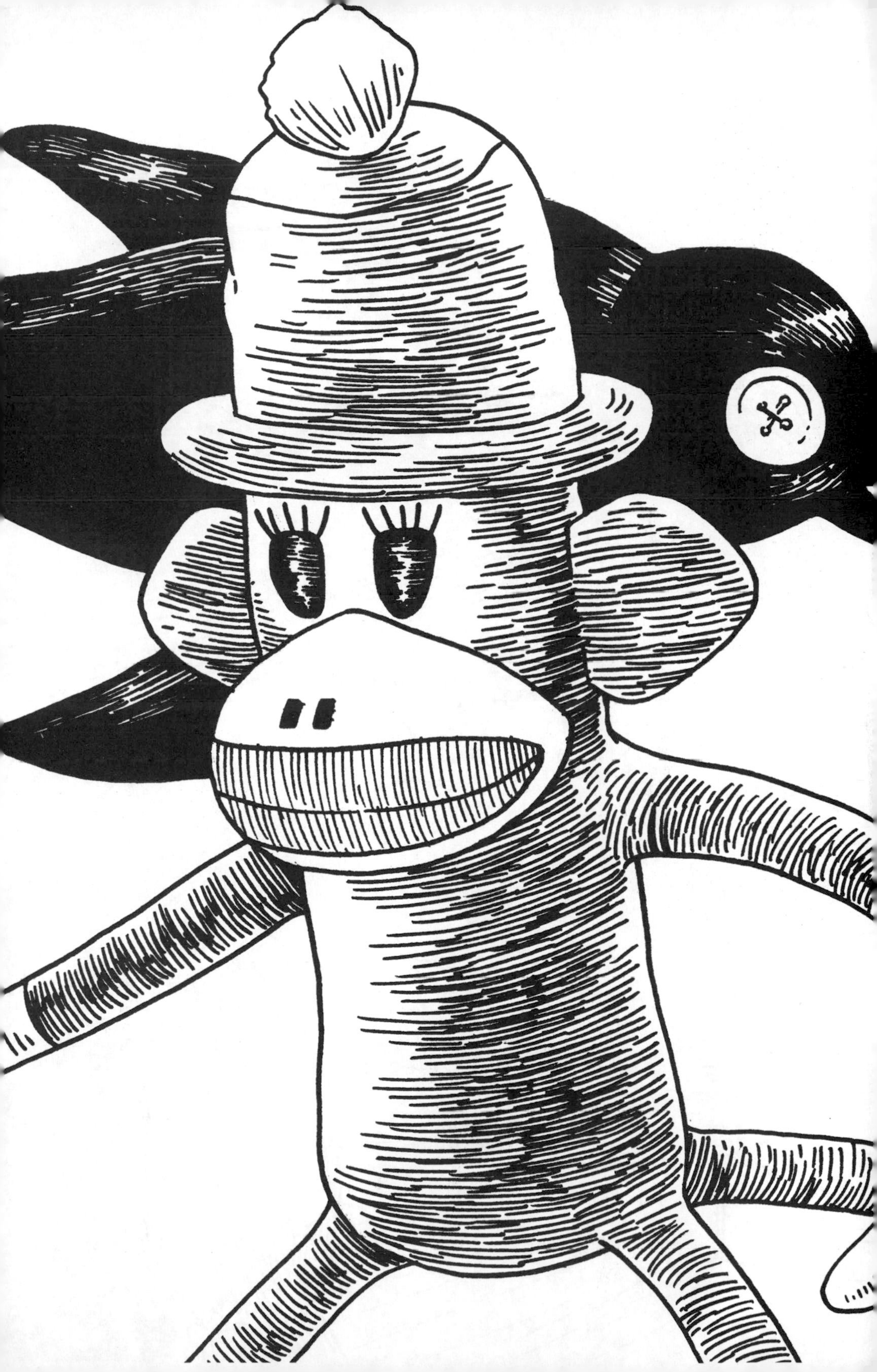

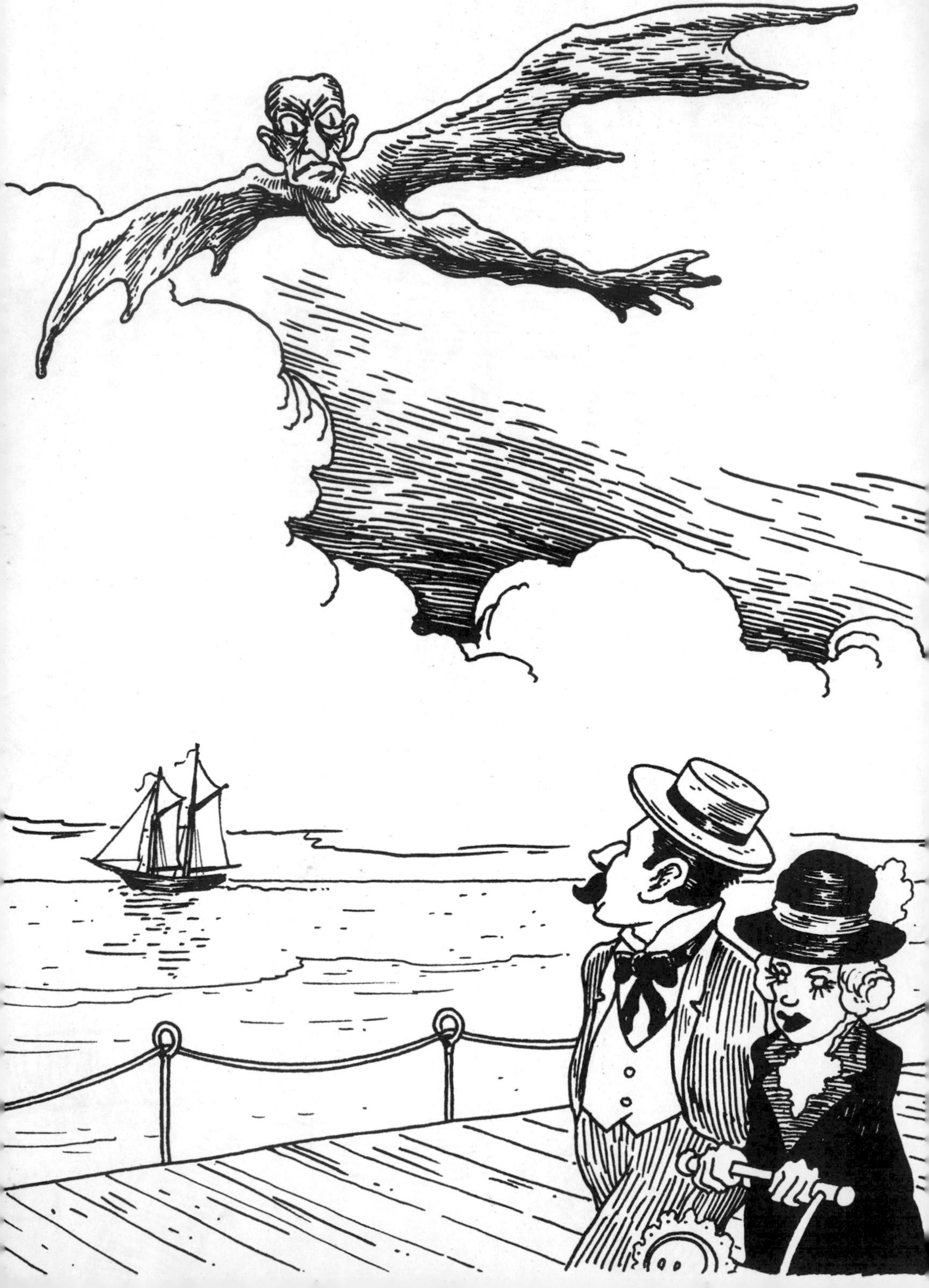